gofish
PROJECT

Where the Church and the World
Intersect to Make a Difference

KERRY FLOWERS

WESTBOW°
PRESS
A DIVISION OF THOMAS NELSON
& ZONDERVAN

WestBow Press books may be ordered through booksellers or by contacting:

WestBow Press
A Division of Thomas Nelson & Zondervan
1663 Liberty Drive
Bloomington, IN 47403
www.westbowpress.com
1 (866) 928-1240

Because of the dynamic nature of the Internet, any web addresses or links contained in this book may have changed since publication and may no longer be valid. The views expressed in this work are solely those of the author and do not necessarily reflect the views of the publisher, and the publisher hereby disclaims any responsibility for them.

Any people depicted in stock imagery provided by Thinkstock are models, and such images are being used for illustrative purposes only.
Certain stock imagery © Thinkstock.

Cover art courtesy Jason Thomas, Inc., at www.jthomas.net

ISBN: 978-1-4908-5919-4 (sc)
ISBN: 978-1-4908-5920-0 (hc)
ISBN: 978-1-4908-5918-7 (e)

Library of Congress Control Number: 2014920467

Printed in the United States of America.

WestBow Press rev. date: 11/14/2014

To him who is able to do immeasurably more than all
we ask or imagine, according to his power that is at work
within us, to him be glory in the church and in Christ Jesus
throughout all generations, for ever and ever! Amen.
Ephesians 3:20

Contents

Acknowledgments

One winter night in 2008, I sat alone at my desk. An idea gripped me so tightly that I had to sketch it out while it was fresh in my mind. That idea eventually became the book you are reading—*The Go Fish Project*.

Even before 2008, the Go Fish Project was percolating in my mind thanks to the following people.

My parents—Bud and Ina Flowers—modeled for me that church is not a place to go and sit but rather an opportunity to go and serve. I learned the Go Fish Project values of simple social service from watching them as a child … and today, as an adult, I still see my parents living these values daily.

You'll meet my siblings, Kirk and Kelly, in the book, but those stories only paint a small picture of the lessons, experience, and wisdom I gained from them as the third of three children. Usually the last child learns from the mistakes of his older siblings. I learned pretty quickly that the easiest path for me would be to just follow their example.

Youth ministers Dave Campbell and Bryce Cox fanned the flame to use my gifts and talents to reach a lost world in my own unique fashion. Football coaches Lester Smith and Bud Pigott showed me that leaders can be fierce competitors without compromising spiritual integrity. J. C. and Pat Herring taught a whole generation of young married couples at Dawson Memorial Baptist Church how to juggle life and live for Christ.

Since 2008, *The Go Fish Project* has been helped along by several people.

Six friends in particular gathered at Fairhope Inn one night to discuss the idea and an early manuscript. Letia Seaborn was the sergeant at arms who kept us on task that evening, or tried to, as we walked through the idea. Her husband, Robert, sat at the table that night without his reading glasses and was thus relegated to making jokes and drawing the ire of the sergeant at arms. Traci Watson, upon receiving the manuscript for the first time, immediately began to correct the material in lieu of dessert. And her husband, Ralph Watson, sampled everyone's dessert in lieu of discussing the manuscript. Genie Bailey furiously made notes while we finished eating so that later she could group text everyone with ideas and opinions at 11:15 p.m. And her husband, Owen Bailey, silently corrected my grammar while I was explaining the book—eagerly awaiting his red pen to start the editing process on paper. These six friends willingly lent a hand to review a book, yes, but would have done much more if asked—and they did. I count these friends among the many blessings I do not deserve.

Chief among blessings that I do not deserve is my wife, Christy. I truly don't think you would be reading this book had I not married her. I would have never risked it had I not felt her support. Her approach to life is creative; she prefers to figure things out as she goes along. To her, mistakes are simply learning experiences, and the worst mistake of all is not attempting something new. In that environment, I felt inspired and free to pursue a dream … again. The first time I pursued a dream has also been successful—when she became my wife.

Introduction

If I look at the mass, I will never act. If I look at the one, I will.
—Mother Teresa

This book was written to create a movement—a movement by Christians to change the world. The world needs changing, and there's nobody more qualified to change it for the better than Christians. But let's not get carried away. Changing the world is a mighty big ambition for a group that is shrinking in size, is dwindling in participation, and is outdated, out of touch, and closed-minded, according to the mainstream media.

If you asked the casual observer what the role of the church is in today's society, I'm not sure he could give you one. Even worse, I'm not sure the casual *church member* could give you one! For a multitude of reasons, Christians are on the outside looking in when it comes to influencing and impacting our world.

But ... as long as we have Christ, we have hope.

Some say the world is too far gone. Our burdens are heavy just protecting ourselves—our families, our spouses, our kids—from this present darkness. I would agree with you. First Peter 5:8–9 says, "Be self-controlled and alert! Your enemy the devil prowls around like a roaring lion looking for someone to devour. Resist him, standing firm in the faith, because you know that your brothers throughout the world are undergoing the same kind of suffering."

Did you catch that last phrase? *Your brothers throughout the world are undergoing the same kind of suffering ...*

The way for us *all* to combat this evil is to return to Christ, whose burden is easy and whose yoke is light. Darkness will retreat when the army of the Lord mobilizes. Imagine what millions of Christians could do if we truly humbled ourselves and united to demonstrate the love of Christ.

But the task *is* rather daunting. How can we reverse our culture where political correctness blots out common sense? Where a broken system of entitlement chokes responsibility? Where good is spun as evil by the media and evil is spun as good? Where right and wrong are relative depending on whom you ask? And where God—once the foundation of society—is not even allowed in our midst anymore?

Somehow, somewhere we lost our way. Christian men and women were once seen as pillars of society. Now we are seen as nuisances. Once we were known for our compassion and caring. Now we are known for our complaining. To reverse this, we need a fresh start. We need to update our image—to rebrand ourselves, so to speak. We cannot do that by sitting on the sidelines. We must wade into the fray and make a difference—one person at a time.

Our gradual slide from the center of society to where we are now on the periphery actually began over one hundred years ago. It was well documented by David Moberg in his 1972 book *The Great Reversal: Evangelism versus Social Concern*. Early churches, particularly in England and America, were noted for their social involvement and for establishing schools for immigrants, homes for unwed mothers, city missions, and the Salvation Army.[1] The great reversal simply refers to the trend of Christians in the early 1900s to focus on evangelism only instead of including social concern with personal salvation.

It is important for Christians to note that the great reversal *preceded* the welfare state in America. The New Deal measures by President Roosevelt in the 1930s and President Johnson's War on Poverty in the 1960s were not the government seeking control.[2] They were government stepping in where the church should have been.

Improvements aimed at society without Christ at the center, however, are hollow. The proof is that while people are being "helped" more than ever before, our society continues its downward spiral.

Sounds too big to overcome, doesn't it? Maybe with our own frail power it is. But don't we still belong to the one who created all things? Isn't he capable? Doesn't he want to help? The answer is a resounding yes, and it is for that reason that Go Fish Project was created. Maybe we are thinking too big here, but two thousand years ago, eleven disciples changed the world.

Imagine the impact millions of like-minded Christians could have if we laid aside our fears, our differences, and our excuses to boldly engage the

---

1 David O. Moberg, *The Great Reversal: Evangelism Versus Social Concern.* (Philadelphia, PA: Lippincott, 1972).
2 Steve Corbett and Brian Fikkert, *When Helping Hurts: How to Alleviate Poverty Without Hurting the Poor ... and Yourself.* (Chicago: Moody Publishers, 2009).

world. Lives would be changed, addictions overcome, marriages reunited, families restored, the weak made strong, and orphans nurtured and widows supported. Hope would absorb fear. Love would overwhelm hate. Evil would be pushed back, and light would brighten the world. Think about it. If we united as a living, breathing body and did what we were created to do, the world would feel the love of Christ. And Jesus, watching from heaven, would smile as his brothers and sisters finally realized their part in the Father's plan of redemption.

Go Fish Project is for individuals who want to participate in something meaningful—who want to make a difference. It is for those who want to be doers of the Word and join like-minded others to design their own ministry projects to impact their communities.

Go Fish Project provides a way for churches to integrate visitors and new members into a welcoming fellowship. For existing members, Go Fish Project will develop a spiritual breadth and depth to rekindle their urgency to demonstrate Christ's love to a very lost world.

With that said, the following is the philosophy behind Go Fish Project.

Our Vision: To change the world.

Our Purpose: To position the church to demonstrate the love of Christ.

- Our Values: *Simple. Social. Service.*

- *Simple*: "Love the Lord your God with all your heart, with all your soul, and with all your mind. This is the greatest and most important command. The second is like it: love your neighbor as yourself" (Matthew 22:37–39).

- *Social*: "Father, as you sent me into the world, I am also sending them into the world" (John 17:18).

- *Service*: "For I was hungry and you gave me something to eat; I was thirsty and you gave me something to drink; I was a stranger and you took me in; I was naked and you clothed me; I was sick and you took care of me; I was in prison and you visited me" (Matthew 25:35–36).

So how do we pull off something this big with the odds stacked against us? We lean upon the grace provided by our Lord Jesus, who, despite our flaws, weaknesses, and sin, can still use us to bring about his glory. And in faith, we go make something happen.

Go Fish Project is a forty-day spiritual renewal and growth process for individuals and churches. The forty-day period is to allow small groups to create, design, and implement their own personalized mission project. The Go Fish Project will direct team members over this period of time on how to significantly impact their communities by demonstrating the love of Christ. And because Go Fish Project is repeatable, relevant, and real, it can become a regular part of individual or church spiritual growth!

So what is Go Fish Project? Let's walk through Go Fish Project step by step so you can understand how easy it is to make a difference!

Who: There are two very important *whos* you will have to identify for Go Fish Project.

1. *Your Team:* Your Go Fish Project team should consist of eight to twelve people who are willing to commit to forty days of spiritual growth that culminates with a mission project in your community. The group size must be kept to eight to twelve for Go Fish Project to work best. The reason? Keeping the group size manageable means that every team member has to get involved and contribute. Participation ensures that each person has a chance to experience the joy of helping others. For example, if you are doing Go Fish Project as part of a small group and there are twenty-four people in your group, you'll need to break up into at least two groups. Or if you are doing it as part of a church effort, it is highly recommended that you organize the groups of eight to twelve around your small group structure (i.e., Sunday school, life groups, etc.). If a small group has over twenty people, it is highly recommended that you create two separate groups with two separate projects.

2. *Partner:* Your team will be asked to identify a partner for your group. The reason your Go Fish Project includes a partner is so the focus is on building relationships, not necessarily just completing a project. As you think about identifying your partner, you may want to keep these things in mind:

- Your partner needs to be someone in the community who is not on your team of eight to twelve people.

- Your partner can be the actual person who your team will help.

- Your partner may also be the point person to get your team into the community so that you can serve. For example, if you discover a need to teach English in a Hispanic neighborhood, seek a willing representative from that neighborhood to assist you in your project. Or if your team uncovers a need to help cancer patients take care of their hair, find a hairdresser who is willing to join your project.

- Your partner may be poor but can very well be someone who is just down on his or her luck at the moment. Go Fish Project talks a lot about the poor and oppressed, but your team has the ultimate decision on who you think is appropriate to target.

What: Go Fish Projects can be as creative as your team can be. Remember, the goal is *not* to select a project before you ever have your first team meeting. Rather the project should be a natural response to the relationships within your team and eventually your partner. The team meetings will help flesh out the exact nature of the project as well as prayer and reflection. That being said, here are some examples that might get you thinking:

- neighborhood block party for the underprivileged

- clothing a neighborhood for winter or the upcoming school year

- teaching the elderly how to operate a computer, iPad, or smartphone

- teaching a language or school tutoring

- CPR, first aid, or nutrition classes

- helping the unemployed find work through training, job skills, interviewing

- taking art or music to the underprivileged or sick

- providing hope for the homeless with meals, temporary work, etc.

- home repair or projects for those who cannot do it themselves

- care packages for hospitalized, sick children, foster kids

How: This book will serve not only as the source for your five team meetings but also as a personal devotional guide to keep you moving over the duration of your project. The daily devotionals, in turn, will prepare you for the team meetings and give you some needed insight on how to deliver your Go Fish Project in the best way in your community.

The forty days will include five team meetings. The first four meetings will be held weekly as part of your church's small group training, as a Wednesday-night prayer meeting, or as just a weekly Bible study. It makes no difference how you structure it. The goal is to bring together your team on a weekly basis to discuss, plan, and implement the project. The fifth and last meeting is a celebration to be held once your Go Fish Project is complete. Here are the guidelines for the team meetings each week:

Team Meeting 1—*Prepare*: Before you venture out into the community, there are some things you must know. This week is to put you in the right mind-set as you go.

Team Meeting 2—*Partner*: This is where Go Fish Project differs from many short-term mission projects. We want to avoid the paternalism that exists in most efforts where the church swoops in with resources and directs the work from start to finish. We want you to seek the Lord's guidance on *who* to partner with so your partner can in turn recruit local help and talent for collaboration. Hint: Pray about this. Don't rush the Holy Spirit. Allow him to guide your decision on who your partner will be.

Team Meeting 3—*Plan*: Now that you have a partner, collaboration is necessary for you to organize your Go Fish Project. By the end of this meeting, not only will your team have a blueprint for what to do, but you will also be well on your way to building relationships in the community.

Team Meeting 4—*Perform*: With everyone on board, this meeting is to put final organizational plans in place for your project. If you are still planning, that is fine, but don't wait too much longer. Continue to build relationships as you go out and implement your project.

Team Meeting 5—*Praise*: As you complete your first Go Fish Project, a celebration is necessary! Take time to praise God, thank your partner, thank your team, and party! It is highly recommended that you debrief your team and your partner(s) to learn how to improve upon this experience and prepare yourself for your next Go Fish Project!

When: The only timetable for the Go Fish Project is the forty-day implementation period. This ensures that the momentum is sustained and there is a sense of urgency to complete the task. Group meetings and the actual project are left up to you to coordinate and schedule.

Where: We do have one rule for implementing your Go Fish Project. It must be done within your community. Why? Growing churches have this in common: they understand how to extend the church in socially relevant ways into their communities.

Why: The purpose is to position the church to demonstrate the love of Christ and in doing so, change the world!

The Forty Days of the Go Fish Project

Prepare Days 1-7	• Are you ready? Preparing your heart to go out into the community • Hold Team Meeting One, then do daily evotionals 1-7
Partner Days 8-14	• Whom shall we send? Deciding on a Go Fish Partner • Hold Team Meeting Two, then continue daily devotionals 8-14
Plan Days 15-21	• What shall we do? Collaborating with community partner on GFP plan • Hold Team Meeting Three, continue daily devotionals 15-21
Perform Days 22-35	• Implement Go Fish Project...Team/Partner go out into community • Hold Team Meeting Four, continue daily devotionals 22-35 while you go...
Praise Days 36-40	• Celebrate! Team & Partner celebrate the completion of their GFP! • Celebration is Team Meeting Five; finish daily devotionals 36-40; repeat GFP!

WEEK 1

Week 1—Prepare

Team Meeting 1

One of the characteristics of the Go Fish Project (GFP) that makes it unique is that we want you to be fully engaged and in charge of the process. For that reason, you will notice that the structure of the GFP is simultaneously rigid and flexible. The more rigid parts of the GFP are meant to keep the process on track, such as the steps of the team meetings and the flow of the daily devotionals. The more flexible parts are to allow you to determine your team's unique signature on the project, such as who leads your team meetings, who you choose as a partner, what project fits your team, how long it takes to do your project, and what type of celebration you choose as you finish your project. So, here's your first choice: pick some lucky individual to lead your first team meeting!

Step 1   Pick one passage from each column, and have someone read it aloud to the group. It doesn't matter which set of verses you read; just read one from each column.

Revelation 4:1–11	Job 38
Exodus 33:12–23	Psalm 139:1–18
Isaiah 40:10–22	Revelation 19:1–16
Exodus 14:10–22	Revelation 5:1–14

Discuss the magnificence, the power, the might, and the abilities of our almighty God that are described in the passages you read.

1.   What excites you when you read these passages?

2.   Because of his presence and power, we cannot see God in our present state and live! What do you think you will do when you can see him face-to-face in heaven?

1

3. What would happen if churchgoers realized the power that was available to them and united to demonstrate the love of Christ to our world?

Step 2 Discuss a traumatic event that happened in the past (which can include natural events, such as a hurricane, tornado, earthquake, tsunami, fire, flood, or blizzard, or man-made events, such as the September 11 terrorist attacks). Specifically, discuss your memories around the following things:

1. What was the mind-set of neighbors helping neighbors?

2. What do you remember about the sacrifices people made for each other?

3. How did your neighborhood or community come together during this time?

What you've just discussed—the coming together, the unselfish acts, the kindness, the hyper-focus on what is truly important—that is what we want to recreate through the Go Fish Project. But instead of waiting on a natural disaster, we are going to do it in your community in the next forty days.

Step 3 Review what you will do during the forty days of the Go Fish Project.

Team

Each week you will have a team meeting to plan, organize, and discuss your project. The team meeting will be your chance to collaborate as teammates on the project but also to develop a relationship with someone in your community. We encourage all team members to attend the weekly team meetings so you can keep up—we will be moving fast!

Individual

Over the forty days of the Go Fish Project, daily devotionals will encourage team members and prepare them for the weekly team meetings. The devotionals will also lead you to a deeper understanding of the Christian's place in the world and why we are gifted to demonstrate Christ's love as part of our witness. The devotionals will contain a story, a Scripture, a prayer guide, and something we are calling the 5:10 task. More about that on your first daily devotional!

Step 4   Before you leave today, please do the following:

Team

1. Take a team photo, and have a team member who is tech savvy upload your photo on the Go Fish Project website (www.gofishproject.com). While uploading your photo, take a few minutes to enter your team's information so you can see how your team and others are making an impact in different areas around the world.

2. Schedule the next three team meetings on your calendars. We highly recommend scheduling around normal church activities to increase participation. Team meetings are designed to last no more than sixty minutes. (The fifth team meeting can be scheduled at a later date as it will serve as a celebration upon the completion of your project.)

3. Using the inventory worksheet in the appendix, write down an inventory of the personal and professional experience of the members on your team. Your group will refer back to this in a future team meeting. Please note that there are fourteen rows on the table—one to serve as an example, twelve for your Go Fish Project team, and one for your partner. Your partner will complete his/her inventory during the third team meeting.

Step 5   Come together in prayer. Pray specifically for the following things:

1. That the name of our God be glorified

2. That the Holy Spirit be present throughout the project in order to prepare team members for their roles, to help your team identify those to whom your missionary project will cater to, and to reveal God's presence throughout the project

3. That the bride of Christ—his church—be strengthened by your project.

Not So Fast, My Friend!

ESPN's Lee Corso has a flair for the dramatic. Every Saturday morning in the fall, he can be seen debating Kirk Herbstreit, Desmond Howard, and Chris Fowler on ESPN's *College GameDay*. As the show progresses, Corso gets more and more animated, and he works the fans gathered around the set into a frenzy. By the end of each *GameDay*, he either delights or disgusts the home crowd by donning the mascot's headgear for the team he picks to win.

Of all his antics, my favorite is when Corso delivers his famous quip, "Not so fast, my friend!" This statement is reserved for his fellow ESPN analysts when Corso is in sharp disagreement with them. He then points out the error of their ways and backs it up with proof.

Through his prophet Isaiah, God told his people the same thing.

The people believed they were doing what was right: worshipping God, even fasting to show their commitment to him. And the Lord said through Isaiah, "Not so fast, my friend!"

As you read the Scriptures for today, look carefully at the sharp disagreement with what the people were doing and what the Lord required. I'm afraid that if I am honest with myself, I am guilty as charged, just like the Israelites.

As you begin the Go Fish Project, start today by preparing yourself. The world you will enter desperately needs to see the truth. Get ready to show the world what the truth—God—looks like.

Week 1: Prepare

Reflection: Neither churches nor individuals need another project; what we need is to go back to our purpose.

Scripture: Isaiah 58:5–7, 10

Is this the kind of fast I have chosen, only a day for people to humble themselves? Is it only bowing one's head like a reed and for lying in sackcloth and ashes? Is that what you call a fast, a day acceptable to the Lord? Is not this the kind of fasting I have chosen: to loosen the chains of injustice and untie the cords of the yoke, to set the oppressed free and break every yoke? Is it not to share your food with the hungry and to provide the poor wanderer with shelter— when you see the naked, to clothe them and not to turn away from your own flesh and blood? ... If you spend yourselves on behalf of the hungry and satisfy the needs of the oppressed, then your light will rise in the darkness, and your night will become like the noonday.

Pray/Meditate:

1. Dwell on these verses for a few minutes. Ask the Lord to point out where we have sinned as a nation as stewards of his church.

2. Ask the Lord through his Spirit to speak to you about your worship and fasting. Are they up to his standards? Where can you repent?

3. Look at verse 10. Our world is a dark place. Allow yourself to envision how great it would be if Christians united to spread light. Spend a moment imagining what that might look like in your community.

5:10 Task: Each day the devotional will contain a simple task to perform. Don't worry—they are fast, fun, and enjoyable. We call it our 5:10 task. Why? Luke 5:10 reads, "Don't be afraid; from now on you will be fishers of men!"

That's what the Go Fish Project is all about! To make it memorable, we suggest a reminder at 5:10 a.m. or 5:10 p.m. every day for the duration of the Go Fish Project. So today, your task is to set a reminder or alarm for the next forty days on your cell phone to perform your 5:10 task. The reminder can be set for either 5:10 a.m. or 5:10 p.m.—whichever you prefer.

Be the Person Your Dog Thinks You Are

One summer evening several years ago, my wife asked me to grill hamburgers for supper. Her hamburgers are a family favorite, seasoned to perfection. And since we have three teenage boys, it usually takes me two hands to flip the sizeable patties.

On this particular night, the burgers were so large that the boys and I were covering up leftover portions with our napkins. So, as not to hurt my wife's feelings, I quickly gathered the boys' chunks of burger onto my plate while she was getting water from the kitchen.

"Wooo—I am full!" I said with a slap to my belly. "Anyone want to give Dudley the leftovers?" Jack, the animal lover in the group, quickly volunteered. And that is when the night became memorable.

Dudley was our eight-year-old English bulldog. By this point, he resembled Helen Keller more than our family pet. He was nearly blind from cataracts, and his hearing was pretty much nil. And to ease our guilt about his condition, we probably gave him way too many hamburger scraps, so besides being nearly blind and deaf, he was also overweight.

Jack and I went to the backyard and leaned over the gate to give Dudley his treats. As usual, he was asleep, snoring loudly. Rousing a deaf and blind English bulldog from sleep is not an easy task, so Jack tossed a piece near his nose so we could rouse him using the only functioning sense he had left. It worked perfectly.

Dudley quickly ate the piece and sniffed around for more. After we engaged in much yelling and slapping the fence, he finally located us and strolled over. I threw a big chunk to him. In retrospect, it was too big.

You see, bulldogs can't breathe that well to begin with, and with a ball of hamburger now obstructing his airway, Dudley was struggling for air. At

8

first Jack and I just laughed because that's the way bulldogs always eat. But we soon realized Dudley was struggling. While he couldn't make the universal sign for choking, we knew he was in trouble.

Just as I put one foot on the fence to hop over, Dudley passed out. His massive frame went limp, and he fell over on his side. The force generated from his weight hitting the ground propelled the bolus of beef a good foot and a half out of his mouth onto our patio. Dudley came to, and shaking his head, he casually ambled over and finished his treat.

Now Jack and I were the ones who couldn't breathe. I've never laughed so hard in my life.

Dudley heard the commotion and walked over to the fence, wagging his nub of a tail. Amazing! I just about killed him and he still thought I was the greatest master ever.

To change the perception of Christians in our world, we have to be the people our dogs think we are: caring, compassionate, and consistent. Dogs can smell a hypocrite, and so can the world.

Are you ready to go fish?

Week 1:	Prepare
Reflection:	Before you go out in the community, look inward.
Scripture:	Isaiah 1:11, 16–17

"The multitude of your sacrifices—what are they to me?" says the Lord. "I have more than enough of burnt offerings, of rams and the fat of fattened animals; I have no pleasure in the blood of bulls and lambs and goats … Wash and make yourselves clean. Take your evil deeds out of my sight; stop doing wrong. Learn to do right; seek justice. Defend the oppressed. Take up the cause of the fatherless; plead the case of the widow."

Pray/Meditate:

1. Praise God for his patience, mercy, and love—traits that distinguish him as the one, true God.

2. Thank him for the true worshippers over thousands of years who have kept his name holy and paved the way for you to be included in his family.

3. Seek forgiveness for the global church, your local church, and yourself for neglecting the pattern of worship outlined in the verses above.

5:10 Task:	Call, e-mail, or text (your choice) a widow, an orphan, or someone who is discouraged or oppressed and encourage him or her.

Does This Dress Make Me Look Fat?

In ancient Greece, debates were all the rage. Acts 17:21 says, "All the Athenians and the foreigners who lived there spent their time doing nothing but talking about and listening to the latest ideas."

During a typical exchange in ancient Greece, orators would attempt to place their opponents in a dilemma that forced them to choose either one option or another. It didn't matter which option the opponent picked—either way he lost the argument.

Today, a rhetorical question might be one we have all heard: "Does this dress make me look fat?"

If you are a married man, red flags should be waving. Warning sirens should be going off. This is a dangerous question. No Greek orator in his right mind would have attempted to answer it!

Rhetorical questions like the one above are not meant to elicit a response but more to present a point. And like the Greek orator's opponent, if you do answer, regardless of your response, you are immediately placed on the horns of a dilemma.

Suppose you took the bait and answered your lady with, "You know, you do look a little chunky in that one, but you still look great." The typical response of most wives would be something like this: "What? Are you saying I'm fat? Do you really think I wanted you to answer that? What could possibly make you think that would make me feel good about myself? There's no way I can go to the party now. I'm sure you don't want to be seen with such a heifer!"

If this ever happens, leave the room quickly. Start vacuuming or cleaning bathrooms, or make a list of possible expensive anniversary gifts and leave it out where she can find it later.

On the other hand, should you take the other position, and say, "No, you look fine," you might hear this response: "You are lying! You don't think I'm smart enough to see that? Maybe if I wasn't taking care of your food, your laundry, and your kids all the time, I could have some time to exercise! What do you think of *that*?"

Men, this is a clever ploy by the woman. She has answered her own rhetorical question with another one just to see if you will make the same mistake twice. Whatever you do, do *not* respond. If you do, discomfort looms.

Since I have been happily married for over twenty-three years, I can confidently say I have no clue how to answer those dilemma-producing rhetorical questions. As a general rule, I have found that peace exists in the home when I am encouraging and supportive. Let the negative stuff come from outside the marriage.

There are times, however, when my wife presses me. When the issue is about character or integrity, she values truth over flattery. She knows that because I love her and care about her future, I will be honest.

As we prepare our hearts to go out and demonstrate the love of Christ, be candid with yourself. Ask yourself, "Am I ready for this?"

The question is not a rhetorical one.

Week 1:   Prepare

Reflection: Seek truth from our Savior.

Scripture: Revelation 3:14–17

> To the angel of the church in Laodicea write: These are the words of the Amen, the faithful and true witness, the ruler of God's creation. I know your deeds, that you are neither cold nor hot. I wish you were either one or the other! So, because you are lukewarm—neither hot nor cold—I am about to spit you out of my mouth. You say, "I am rich; I have acquired wealth and do not need a thing." But you do not realize that you are wretched, pitiful, poor, blind and naked. I counsel you to buy from me gold refined in the fire, so you can become rich; and white clothes to wear, so you can cover your shameful nakedness; and salve to put on your eyes, so you can see.

Pray/Meditate:

1. Ask the Holy Spirit to answer this question: "Do you think I am lukewarm?" Jesus, the faithful and true witness, will answer. Listen quietly for a response.

2. Verse 18 starts with, "I counsel you." The job of a counselor is to lead those counseled to discover the truth. Pray for direction as the Spirit of our Lord counsels you to buy his gold, his clothes, and his salve.

3. Pray that no one has reason to accuse you or your group of hypocrisy.

5:10 Task: Call, text, or e-mail a friend who is a true confidant and thank that friend for his or her honesty.

A Sense of Entitlement

Margaret Thatcher, former prime minister of England, once said, "The problem with socialism is that eventually you run out of other people's money."[3] The United States may not be a socialist country yet ... but we have certainly taken strides down that path in recent years.

According to a 2013 news article by Steve Tobak, entitlements are two-thirds of our federal budget. Half of all American households rely on government handouts. As you can see from the following statistics, entitlements are not an isolated problem confined to the welfare recipients in the United States—it is a pervasive and malignant disease spreading through our country.

So how did entitlement spending grow a hundredfold in the past fifty years? Why are we neck deep in an entitlement mentality now? Here are a few of the reasons mentioned in Mr. Tobak's article:

- Outrageous compensation of executives, professional athletes, and entertainers; the green monster of envy makes us want what these people have.

- No term limits on politicians; true civil service takes a backseat to greed and self-preservation, so entitlements grow to keep the votes coming.

- Corruption in the entitlement system; when Americans see other Americans receiving entitlements and living beyond their means, they think, *Where's* my *money?*

- No accountability in Washington; the same politicians with no term limits currently enjoy an approval rating of less than 20

---

3 Llew Gardner interview with Margaret Thatcher on February 5, 1976 for *This Week* on Thames TV.

percent, yet Americans are apathetic about cleaning house with our votes because we know the next group will do the same.

- Political correctness; in simple terms, political correctness means that we are attempting to *not offend* anyone with our words and actions. When that becomes the pervasive habit of government (and it has), limiting one group at the expense of another might cost one side some votes, so why don't we placate both sides with some money, perks, or tax breaks?[4]

By now you are probably wondering how this devotion is supposed to bring you closer to God when all I've done so far is raise your blood pressure! It is true that entitlement is a significant problem. It is also true that demonstrating the love of Christ is the perfect solution.

We are under the rule of a powerful government. Christianity is one of many religious choices. We are the minority in terms of population and influence. And we are portrayed as closed-minded. Sound like America to you? Actually, this is the description of Christians in the Roman Empire around AD 360.

The parallel between what is going on right now in the United States and the Roman Empire at that time is uncanny. We can learn a lot from our early Christian brethren. Rather than waiting for someone else to fix society, they approached it head on. They backed up their Christian talk with a compassionate walk. They demonstrated the love of Christ to all people, so much so that the Roman emperor Julian wrote the following to one of his pagan priests around AD 361:

> For it is disgraceful that, when no Jew ever has to beg, and the impious Galileans support not only their own poor but ours as well, all men see that our people lack aid from us.[5]

In other words, the compassion displayed by Christians to *all people* throughout the empire made the Roman government take notice! Early

4   Steve Tobak, "The Truth Behind Our Entitlement Culture," published February 7, 2013, www.foxbusiness.com/business-leaders/2013/02/07truth-behind-our-entitlement-culture/.
5   W. C. Wright, *The Works of Emperor Julian*, 3 volumes. (London: Lieb Classical Library, 1924).

Christians were busy meeting material and spiritual needs and by doing so, changing the world in which they lived. As a matter of fact, soon after the emperor Julian, Christianity became the dominant religion of the Roman Empire from that point on.

The Christians of AD 360 weren't concerned about who was entitled to what. Despite government, wars, taxes, opinions, and overwhelming odds, they simply got busy showing Christ's love. We could learn a lot from them.

If people are waiting for a handout, let's give them the one they *really* need.

Week 1:	Prepare
Reflection:	Complaining isn't the solution … compassion is.
Scripture:	Numbers 11:4–6

The rabble with them began to crave other food, and again the Israelites started wailing and said, "If only we had meat to eat! We remember the fish we ate in Egypt at no cost—also the cucumbers, melons, leeks, onions and garlic. But now we have lost our appetite; we never see anything but this manna!"

Pray/Meditate:

1. Pray over our country. Seek forgiveness for allowing it to sink to such a pitiful moral state.

2. Pray that the church can draw attention to the truth—that the answer for our broken system and broken people is the love of Jesus.

3. Pray specifically for your Go Fish Project—not just that the project would be completed but that lives would be changed.

5:10 Task: Watch the following YouTube clip and avoid being the "me" monster: http://www.youtube.com/watch?v=vymaDgJ7KLg.

<u>Boil the Frog!</u>

Several scientists in the nineteenth century apparently ran out of ideas for brilliant discoveries, so they threw a frog in a pot and heated it up slowly to see if it would jump out. Nobel Prize–winning stuff, I know.

The theory was that if you raised the temperature slowly enough, the frog would sit back, relax, and tolerate extreme temperatures—ultimately dying by being cooked to death. However, if the frog was placed in water that was already boiling, it would immediately attempt to hop to safety.

Later scientists questioned the validity of the frogs and their swimming habits, and the theory has been proven untrue. However, what stuck was a classic metaphor about how humans deal with change. That is, we tolerate gradual change extremely well, but when presented with abrupt or unwanted change, we typically reject it.

Harvard business professor John P. Kotter has dedicated much of his life to the study of change, particularly how leaders handle change and how they manage it. Kotter's research shows that the primary step to produce change is to create a sense of *urgency*.[6] In the experiment mentioned above, boiling water created the urgency for the frogs to jump.

The gradual slide of morals in our society in the last couple of generations has been skillfully positioned as political correctness, tolerance, and open-mindedness. To argue with any of those views paints the opposition as ignorant, phobic, and judgmental. Not wanting to appear out of touch, most Christians have pulled back from society and kept to themselves. This has allowed the moral slide not only to continue but also to pick up momentum. We now find ourselves in the middle of a hot mess.

---

6   John P. Kotter, *Leading Change*. (Boston: Harvard Business School Press, 1996).

To stem the tide, we must create our own sense of urgency. According to Kotter, that sense of urgency should "connect to the deepest values of people and inspire them to greatness."[7]

As Christians, our deepest value should mirror the deepest value of our God—compassion.

Our world longs for heartfelt compassion but seeks it from the wrong sources. When we show genuine compassion toward each other, others gain a brief glimpse of our Lord. More glimpses provide an accurate vision, and with that vision, we can change the world.

But first, I have to ask … is your water boiling yet?

---

7   Ibid., pg. 37.

Week 1:	Prepare
Reflection:	Our urgency should come from the fact that many will spend eternity separated from God.
Scripture:	Revelation 10:9–10

So I went to the angel and asked him to give me the little scroll. He said to me, "Take it and eat it. It will turn your stomach sour, but in your mouth it will be as sweet as honey." I took the little scroll from the angel's hand and ate it. It tasted as sweet as honey in my mouth, but when I had eaten it, my stomach turned sour.

Pray/Meditate:

1. The scroll John ate was sweet with the words of God but bitter because it resulted in the judgment of the nations. Pray for opportunities to show your compassion to lessen the bitterness in our world today.

2. Pray for the church of our Lord to experience a sense of urgency and break our hearts for what breaks his.

3. Think of a family member, friend, or someone you know who is lost. Pray that you may play a compassionate role in this person coming to know our Lord.

5:10 Task: Call, text, or e-mail an unbeliever and invite him or her to church or a church event.

Reversing the Great Reversal

Simply put, the Great Reversal refers to a time in recent history when the global church became divided on how to address the problems that exist in society.

The best way to describe what happened during the Great Reversal is to think of a railroad track. The church, despite being composed of various denominations, was composed of one train, and everyone on board felt the church should be involved in the concerns of society. Thus, the collective church built schools for immigrants and homes for unwed mothers and developed entities like the Salvation Army to care for the body and soul of the needy.

Around 1900 or so, the church train came to a railway switch. The social gospelers, the more liberal portion of the church, continued down the line of involving the church in society's needs. The evangelicals, however, switched tracks and broke off to focus on individual evangelism, thinking the key to shaping society started with the individual.

What formed was, in essence, two trains on different tracks—the Great Reversal. The evangelicals, wanting to distance themselves from the more liberal theology, continued to focus on individual responsibility and accountability to the gospel. The social gospelers persisted with their close involvement with society, although eventually dropping their evangelical efforts. The theological gap widened, and the tracks between the two continued to diverge.

Church members, listen carefully. What I am about to say hurts, but it is unfortunately the truth. The lasting effects of the Great Reversal are now being fully realized. The government and other organizations have stepped in to care for society. People view the church as socially irrelevant. The church operates in a protective mode, further isolating us from the very people who need us. The perception out there is that the church has derailed off the tracks.

In the last thirty years, people have left the church at an alarming rate. Worse, without a meaningful faith, existing members have one foot in the church and one foot in the world rendering their witness ineffective. We are left with people exiting the train at every stop and only a trickle of new passengers coming on board.

For us to continue the same habits and expect different results is the definition of insanity. As Christians, if we are not growing then why do we continue with the same practices? As churches, if we are not creating disciples, then why continue with the same programs or traditions?

We must reverse this Great Reversal by meeting society at its needs rather than trying to draw society to us. How many sermons do we need to hear on Sunday morning, Sunday night, and Wednesday night before *doing* something?

Jesus ate with sinners, Pharisees, tax collectors, and disciples. He addressed physical, social, and spiritual needs of the people he met. If Jesus was a train conductor, he would say as the train left the station, "*All aboard!*"

Shouldn't we?

Week 1:	Prepare

Reflection: Reverse the trend of individualism; help our less fortunate brothers and sisters.

Scripture: James 2:14–17

What good is it, my brothers and sisters, if someone claims to have faith but has no deeds? Can such faith save them? Suppose a brother or a sister is without clothes and daily food. If one of you says to them, "Go in peace; keep warm and well fed," but does nothing about their physical needs, what good is it? In the same way, faith by itself, if it is not accompanied by action, is dead.

Pray/Meditate:

1. Pray that the Holy Spirit will reveal the character of God to you. Meditate on Jesus' example of addressing the rich, the poor, and the sick. What did he do?

2. Pray for your group to experience the Lord anew and that each member would have a fresh encounter with our Lord.

3. Pray for the Holy Spirit to begin to reveal your Go Fish partner.

5:10 Task: During the next twenty-four hours, speak to someone that you normally wouldn't. Make an attempt to understand his or her perspective.

<u>Unroll the Scroll</u>

As a senior in high school, a friend of mine was promised a car if he secured an academic scholarship for college. Sure enough, his grades and ACT score earned him a nice chunk of cash for school, so his parents kept their end of the bargain and purchased him a shiny new car.

There was only one problem: the car had a manual transmission, and despite his 4.0 grade point, he couldn't drive a stick.

He spent the next few days admiring his new car but not driving it. Instead, he searched for a practice car to learn on and not tear up his transmission. One friend reluctantly volunteered, and by the end of that first week, his shifting was as smooth as silk. The timing was perfect too. He wanted to surprise his girlfriend Friday night by showing up in his new car. And since she also drove a stick shift, his execution needed to be flawless.

On Friday night he eased into her driveway to pick her up for the movies. On their way out to the car, she noticed his new ride. "What! When did you get this?" she inquired.

"Earlier this week," he answered. Suddenly, a wave of nervousness passed over him. "You wanna drive?" he asked.

"Oh, no way. I want you to drive me around in your new car!" she said with a smile.

He closed her door and walked around to the driver's side; a bead of sweat was developing on his forehead. Luckily, when he arrived he had positioned the car to simply make a U-turn out of the driveway to head out; he still was a little shaky with reverse.

My friend cranked up the car and whipped around to head out but slightly miscalculated the new car's turning radius and had to slam on brakes before crashing into the mailbox on the other side of the street. To make matters worse, he was on a downhill slope.

Hills were not included in his first week's training.

To get the car to go in reverse, he had to depress the clutch, but that meant the car would roll forward, thus destroying the mailbox, and more importantly, scratching his new car. Another bead of sweat popped up on his forehead. He sat there for what seemed like thirty seconds trying to recall what to do. His mind had nothing to offer, which only made the drama worse.

Finally, he swallowed his pride. "I think I'm stuck," he said sheepishly.

"Here," she said, pulling up the emergency brake. "Try it now."

To his amazement, the car held its ground while he put it in reverse. Once he had sufficient room to navigate, his girlfriend eased the emergency brake back into position. Off they went to see Tom Cruise in *Top Gun*.

What my friend learned that day is something that every person who has owned a car with a manual transmission knows—there is no operating manual for learning how to drive a stick shift. You just have to wing it and learn as you go.

When Jesus was ready to begin his public ministry, however, he didn't wing it. He actually had an operating manual—the Scriptures. Jesus quoted the Old Testament many times, including today's verses in Isaiah on the day he launched his public ministry. He used Isaiah often to emphasize the disconnect between God and his people.

Jesus used Scripture at every turn to navigate his mission. He used his operating manual to shift gears effortlessly as he encountered the Pharisees, the poor, the rich, the crowds, and even Satan.

Jesus read Isaiah that day to describe how he was going to operate on earth. As his followers, shouldn't they describe our efforts too?

Week 1:	Prepare
Reflection:	Jesus preached the good news in word *and* deed—and we should too.
Scripture:	Luke 4:16–21

He went to Nazareth, where he had been brought up, and on the Sabbath day he went into the synagogue, as was his custom. He stood up to read, and the scroll of the prophet Isaiah was handed to him. Unrolling it, he found the place where it is written: "The Spirit of the Lord is on me, because he has anointed me to proclaim good news to the poor. He has sent me to proclaim freedom for the prisoners and recovery of sight for the blind, to set the oppressed free, to proclaim the year of the Lord's favor." Then he rolled up the scroll, gave it back to the attendant and sat down. The eyes of everyone in the synagogue were fastened on him. He began by saying to them, "Today this scripture is fulfilled in your hearing."

Pray/Meditate:

1. Jesus quoted Isaiah 42:7 in today's Scripture, saying that the passage was fulfilled that day in their hearing. What probably gave the worshippers goose bumps is that Isaiah 42:1–6 is clear that the Messiah would be the one doing these things. Thank God for sending Jesus and for providing redemption for you.

2. Spend a good five minutes asking the Holy Spirit to guide you to examples of how Jesus used word and deed in his ministry to preach the good news.

3. This week has been to *prepare* you to go out into the community. Ask the Lord to continue to prepare your heart and soul as we go deeper into Go Fish Project.

5:10 Task: Read Luke 7:22–23. Notice how Jesus described to John the Baptist why he should have faith that he is the Messiah. His ministry included both word *and* deed, just as he said it would that first day he read from Isaiah. Thank God for his faithfulness!

WEEK 2

Week 2—Partner

Team Meeting 2

Step 1   Take a moment and review this week's daily devotions. The emphasis for the week 1 devotions was *preparing your heart to serve*. Was there a particular devotion that stood out this week that someone would like to share with the group?

Step 2   The goal for today's meeting is for your group to identify your Go Fish Project partner. Remember, your partner will be either the actual recipient of your Go Fish Project work or in some cases, the gatekeeper who can open doors in the area of your community that you will serve. Whatever type of partner you choose, the partner will work closely with you from here on out. So let's pause and pray for two things:

    1. For the Holy Spirit to provide clarity to identify the perfect partner

    2. For the eventual partner—that his/her needs will be met and that relationships will be strengthened

Step 3   To help your group determine your Go Fish Project partner, read the following descriptions from poor people about what it is like to actually be poor.

    -   Poverty is pain; it feels like a disease. It attacks a person not only materially but also morally. It eats away one's dignity and drives one into total despair.[8]

    -   We poor people are invisible to others; just as blind people cannot see, they cannot see us.[9]

---

8   Deepa Narayan, et al., *Voices of the Poor: Can Anyone Hear Us?* (New York: Published for the World Bank, Oxford University Press, 2000).
9   Ibid.

- Poverty is humiliation, the sense of being dependent on others and of being forced to accept rudeness, insults, and indifference when we seek help.[10]

- When I don't have [any food to bring my family], I borrow, mainly from neighbors and friends. I feel ashamed standing before my children when I have nothing to help feed the family. I'm not well when I'm unemployed. It's terrible.[11]

- Poverty is lack of freedom, enslaved by crushing daily burden, by depression and fear of what the future will bring.[5]

- The forces of poverty and impoverishment are so powerful today. Governments or the big churches can only manage them. So we now feel somewhat helpless. It is this feeling of helplessness that is so painful, more painful than poverty itself.[12]

- I needed colored pencils for a project once. My teacher told me that if I didn't bring them, I wouldn't be able to do my project and I'd get a zero. I told the teacher I didn't have any, and she told me I'd better figure it out. On the way to school, my mom went into the grocery store. I was confused because she told me she didn't have money. When she came out, she had the pencils, but they were in her purse, not in a sack. I think she stole them. She was crying.[13]

- When I say I am poor, I don't mean that it's going to take me two weeks to save for a new iPad or the next iWhatever. I don't mean that I'll need a coupon to shop at J.Crew. I mean that I have saved my kids' Halloween candy for times when my blood sugar gets too low after a day of not eating because I can't afford

10 Ibid.
11 Ibid.
12 Ibid.
13 Tiffany Willis, *87 Things That Poor Kids Know,* published on Liberal America website, May 2014. http://www.liberalamerica.org/2014/05/29/things-poor-kids-know/.

enough food for three square meals for the entire family.[14]

How did these excerpts alter your thinking about the materially poor people around you? Think about the voices of the poor within your community. Are there any that come to mind within your group? Does a group member have a relationship with someone who might need a hand? If a materially poor person or family doesn't come to mind, what about someone who has just hit a rough patch and needs the support of your group during this time? What about a pressing need within your community that your group can help address? Discuss as a group.

Step 4 Step 3's discussion should have generated several possibilities for your team's Go Fish Project partner. Now review the GFP team inventory that you assimilated last week. Given your inventory, your networks, and your community as a target area, narrow your potential partners for your project. Pray and discuss until you arrive at a decision for your partner.

Step 5 Next week (team meeting 3) will involve a discussion with your partner about the gifts, resources, and abilities your group may tap into while doing your Go Fish Project. Using the gifts and abilities of those you are targeting to help complete the project is called asset-based community development (ABCD). This is consistent with what we learned in our devotional this week—namely, that our Lord has blessed all his creation with diverse gifts such as knowledge, networks, land, intelligence, animals, savings, skills, creativity, etc. ABCD asks the partner (and community):

-   What is right with you?

---

14 http://poorasfolk.com/2014/02/19/jenns-words-living-in-poverty-is-like-being-punched-in-the-face-over-and-over-and-over-on-a-daily-basis/. This blog is a resource for people who need to feed themselves and live with little money.

- What gifts has God given you to improve your life and your neighbors?

- How can we use your gifts and abilities and ours to work together to improve your community?

The effect of asking people, "What gifts do you have?" is profound. It affirms their self-esteem and provides hope by associating a brighter future with their contribution. For us, it allows us to see our Go Fish partner as God does, which helps us overcome our own self-importance.

As you wrap up today's meeting, review the following *four components of asset-based community development* and the question under each component:

1. Understand that the people you identified as potential partners are created by God—just like you and me. And like us, they have gifts, resources, and abilities to offer. Identify these capabilities and skills as you start with your partner.

   Question: How did today's discussion enhance your thinking about having a partner as part of the Go Fish Project?

2. Encourage usage of these internal resources once you get your project up and running.

   Question: How would you feel if you couldn't afford to complete a project but you could contribute? (Contributions do not have to be monetary to be significant!)

3. Look to develop key contacts/relationships within the community to further enhance your effectiveness and draw resources.

   Question: How can you pull in others within the community who are in a position to help?

4. Bring in outside resources as needed, but see what the relationships within the community, possibly other churches, or local businesses can do first.

Question: Why is bringing in outside resources listed last? What does that message convey to your partner in the community?

Pray for your Go Fish partner and the relationships soon to be developed.

Looking forward, designate a team member to invite the Go Fish Project partner you identified during today's discussion to your next team meeting. It is critical that the partner be there so he or or he can provide vital insight to your project.

How Do You Eat an Elephant?

How do you eat an elephant? As the old saying goes, "One bite at a time." The proverb reminds us that large goals, even those that seem overwhelming, can be accomplished by breaking the whole thing down into doable parts. Another way to think about it—start simple.

Apple founder Steve Jobs was well known for eating elephants. In fact, they were a staple of his diet. He once motivated his employees at Apple with the words, "Let's put a dent in the universe." Saying that and doing that are two very different things, however.

Jobs's brilliance was that he took complex technology and made it simple for the rest of us.

When Jobs returned to revive a floundering Apple in 1997, he focused the company to deliver on its marketing campaign: *Think Different*. The delivery would come via a new generation of personal computers—the Mac. It was his first elephant.

Jobs was a stickler for details, so when Apple was preparing to launch the Mac, he wanted the perfect name.

Ken Segall, marketing guru and Apple consultant at the time, recalls what Jobs said: "We are betting the company on this, so it needs a great name. It's a full-powered Mac, so it can do a lot of things. But first and foremost, it will get you onto the internet in 10 minutes, even if you've never used a computer before."[14]

The marketing team got the message. Jobs wanted to stress the connection between the Internet and the Mac; thus, the name iMac was born—simple product with a simple name that changed the world. And it all started with a little "i."

As part of the Go Fish Project, you may think, *How can our small group demonstrate the love of Christ enough to make a difference in our community? How can we change the perception of the church? How can we change the world?* What you are really asking is, "How can we eat this elephant?"

It all starts with a little i ... you. Do your part and watch what happens. Remember, a lot of little i's *can* eat an elephant![15]

15   Ken Segall, *Insanely Simple*. (New York: Penguin Group, 2012).

Week 2: Partner

Reflection: Be faithful. Use your little iSelf and be obedient.

Scripture: Numbers 14:6–9

Joshua son of Nun and Caleb son of Jephunneh, who were among those who had explored the land, tore their clothes and said to the entire Israelite assembly, "The land we passed through and explored is exceedingly good. If the Lord is pleased with us, he will lead us into that land, a land flowing with milk and honey, and will give it to us. Only do not rebel against the Lord. And do not be afraid of the people of the land, because we will devour them. Their protection is gone, but the Lord is with us. Do not be afraid of them."

Pray/Meditate:

1. Ten spies saw an elephant. Joshua and Caleb saw a buffet. Pray for the faith, courage, and passion that Joshua and Caleb demonstrated to the people of Israel.

2. Pray for the Holy Spirit to reveal areas in your life where you are overwhelmed and possibly afraid. Spend some time filling your soul with the peace and power of God to overcome your fear.

3. The elephant is large, but our God is bigger. Pray Ephesians 3:20–21 aloud as you close out your prayer time.

5:10 Task: Instead of eating an elephant, fast for one meal today or tomorrow and pray for the other little i's of Go Fish Projects around the world.

Veni, Vedi, Vici

When the weather warmed each spring and summer, Julius Caesar dusted off his shield and polished his breastplate. He sharpened his sword and rolled out his maps. Like the great ones before him, Caesar understood that military might meant power and control.

As the victories piled up, Julius Caesar eventually tired of the laurel wreath headband given to the triumphant general; he had a closet full. He was bored with ticker-tape parades along the Appian Way. His ambition was the purple and gold toga of an emperor.

So after cleaning up Europe and consolidating Rome's standing in Egypt, in the summer of 47 BC, Caesar headed off for Pontus (modern Turkey) to silence a thorn in the Republic's side—Pharnaces.

With legions of battle-tested warriors ready to silence the pesky Pharnaces, Julius Caesar amassed his troops near Xena. The battle was swift and decisive. Upon his return to Rome, it is reported that Caesar provided this succinct description of the skirmish to the Senate: *Veni, vedi, vici.* Translation: I came, I saw, I conquered.

Julius Caesar used the momentum from this victory to assert himself as leader of the Roman Republic. He crushed the foes of the Roman Republic and eliminated his adversaries from within. By 47 BC, Julius Caesar reached his goal; he donned the purple and gold toga of the emperor.

By March 15, 44 BC, however, Julius Caesar was dead—assassinated by a coup.

Power is an elusive, temporary achievement. Control is its cousin. Julius Caesar fought for power and control to establish his kingdom—which lasted for about thirty-six months. Before we trash Caesar for his pride and thirst for power, aren't we all little Caesars? Don't we think that with just a little veni, vidi, vici we can secure our jobs, keep us safe, and provide for the future?

In contrast, notice the pursuits of the early church in Acts 2:

1. They devoted themselves to the common causes of teaching, fellowship, and prayer

2. They shared food, fellowship, fun, and funds

3. They were transparent—no cloak-and-dagger power plays

4. They praised God with glad and sincere hearts

5. They didn't care about money, power, or control

Early Christians witnessed the power and control struggles in the Roman Empire firsthand. They understood, however, that everlasting power originated from God and God alone. They humbled themselves and relinquished control—letting the Lord establish their path.

When we act like this, God comes, he sees, and he conquers the foes before us. As a result, the church—which has lasted a lot longer than Julius Caesar—is built upon the rock.

Week 2:	Partner

Reflection: Go Fish Project is not about what you accomplish but rather what God can accomplish through you.

Scripture: Acts 2:42–47

They devoted themselves to the apostles' teaching and to fellowship, to the breaking of bread and to prayer. Everyone was filled with awe at the many wonders and signs performed by the apostles. All the believers were together and had everything in common. They sold property and possessions to give to anyone who had need. Every day they continued to meet together in the temple courts. They broke bread in their homes and ate together with glad and sincere hearts, praising God and enjoying the favor of all the people. And the Lord added to their number daily those who were being saved.

Pray/Meditate:

1. What it must have been like to be a part of that early church fellowship! Spend a moment reviewing and reflecting on today's verses. Pray that the Holy Spirit will provide insight on what it must have been like in that first church.

2. Pray for the individuals on your team to come together as one to demonstrate the love of Christ in a manner that pleases him.

3. Soon your team will be reaching out to a partner from outside your group to join your team. Pray that your attitude will be like that of the early church.

5:10 Task: Call, text, or e-mail a former team member of yours and rehash some old memories. It could be a former team member from your athletic, band, or cheerleading days. It could be even be a former coworker. Feel the satisfaction that comes from sharing and spreading the glory of past victories with another.

What Happens When Mothers Become Grandmothers?

I never had the pleasure of really knowing my grandmothers. Both of them died when I was very little, so my memories of them are sketchy at best. Somewhere in the deep recesses of my mind, I do recall that my maternal grandmother gave us grandkids a single stick of Fruit Stripe gum in our birthday cards. Part of me remembers the excitement of trying to guess what color the stripes would be on the stick of gum. Another part of me was thinking, *Gee, Grandma, you think you could spring for a whole pack of gum next time?*

Since that was my only memory of a grandmother, imagine my surprise and confusion when my mother became a grandmother. Let me explain.

My mother was this frugal woman who bought one pair of slightly oversized jeans for me at the beginning of each school year. Those same jeans were cut off in May to serve as my summer shorts/bathing suit. Of course, each summer I grew, so that by August I was basically wearing Daisy Dukes. Despite peer ridicule and considerable chafing, we could not purchase a new pair until the week before school started. That was the rule.

And speaking of rules, my mother was the enforcer. She kept a strict schedule of calendars, curfews, and commitments. We adhered to a philosophy of personal responsibility and accountability. Step out of line and face consequences.

With jaw set and blazing green eyes, she could correct without a word. A snap of the fingers and a finger point produced tachycardia and sweat beads. She never had to say, "Just wait until your father gets home," because he was on our side—we were all scared to death!

So what happened to this woman?

Sydney, the first grandchild in our family, was born.

She got more stuff for her first birthday than I did my entire childhood. She got the collector's edition *Little Mermaid* on DVD. We were still watching videos on Beta at our house. She had enough Cabbage Patch kids to make coleslaw for years. She sat in her red and yellow Little Tikes Sporty Coupe even though she barely had enough motor control to keep her head from crashing into the dashboard.

My siblings and I were appalled at the haul from that first birthday. The poor kid was so exhausted from opening all the gifts she couldn't even muster the strength to blow out the only candle on her cake. By the end of that first birthday, Sydney expressed her gratitude with a full-blown fit that was described as "precious and spirited" by her new grandmother. Had we been so precious and spirited as kids, our neighborhood friends would have checked the obituaries the next day just to make sure we survived the night.

As more grandkids were born on both sides of the family, however, I noticed a disturbing trend. The strange case of my mother turning from Mrs. Hyde to Dr. Jekyll was not an isolated occurrence. It was an epidemic.

Mothers everywhere lose their edge upon becoming grandmothers. A penny saved is a penny earned became, "Oh, I've got to get her this outfit for Arbor Day." Arbor Day ... really? Gone was the eye of the tiger, replaced by Mr. Rogers—or worse—Barney!

After much thought, I concluded that grandmothers figure it out faster than the rest of us: we all need to feel compassion. Grandchildren just happen to be their first victims.

Week 2:	Partner
Reflection:	Shower compassion, slower correction—Grandmothers know how to build relationships.
Scripture:	Colossians 1:15–20

The Son is the image of the invisible God, the firstborn over all creation. For in him all things were created: things in heaven and on earth, visible and invisible, whether thrones or powers or rulers or authorities; all things have been created through him and for him. He is before all things, and in him all things hold together. And he is the head of the body, the church; he is the beginning and the firstborn from among the dead, so that in everything he might have the supremacy. For God was pleased to have all his fullness dwell in him, and through him to reconcile to himself all things, whether things on earth or things in heaven, by making peace through his blood, shed on the cross.

Pray/Meditate:

1. Read the verses above slowly, and reflect on the supremacy of our Lord Jesus. God was pleased to shower compassion on a lost and broken world by sending Jesus as Reconciler. Stop a moment and ask the Holy Spirit to use you and your group in the same fashion as you go out into your community.

2. Relationships are a natural by-product of spending time together or working on a project as your group is doing. Pray that the relationships established will reflect God's character and point others toward Him.

3. Pray for a compassionate heart as you find your eventual partner for your project. Remember, you too were in need of compassion before you answered God's call.

| **5:10 Task:** | Call, text, or e-mail a grandmother today. Ask her about her grandkids, but make sure you have allotted plenty of time … |

42

What Is Your Relationship Status?

These days, relationship statuses are all the rage. Social media can announce, update, and display your relationship information 24–7. Without question, the Internet has revealed and expanded our ability to connect with one another through relationships.

If you aren't in a relationship, don't fret! The Internet can help there too.

Currently there are well over one hundred websites to help those seeking a relationship to find one. Several websites tout a compatibility test or formula that will help you find that perfect match for the love of your life.

So why all the fuss about relationship status? It's simple. These websites are capitalizing on a universal truth—the key to a happy life is healthy relationships. We were made to experience life through relationships. When they are missing or damaged or unfulfilled, we seek ways to fill the void.

That said, God's design is for humans to engage in four distinct relationships.[16, 17]

God: He is the center of all relationships—it starts with him. The entire Old Testament tells the story of his yearning to relate to his people. And of course, the New Testament gives us Jesus—God's ultimate display to reconcile us to him.

Others: God said it is not good for man to be alone. We were made to love, support, and encourage each other to seek God's will for our lives.

---

16   Bryant Myers. *Walking with the Poor: Principles and Practices of Transformational Development.* (Maryknoll, NY: Orbis Books, 1999), 27.
17   Steve Corbett and Brian Fikkert. *When Helping Hurts: How to Alleviate Poverty Without Hurting the Poor ... and Yourself.* (Chicago: Moody Publishers, 2009), 54–55.

Jesus commanded us to love our neighbors. Paul urged us to be devoted to one another in brotherly love.

Creation: In Genesis God created us to be fruitful and multiply over the earth but also to take care of it. We are to use the earth and all that is in it to properly manage God's property.

Yourself: If we believe that we were created in God's image, then we are not accidents! We have special worth and a purpose. When our relationship with God, others, and his creation is right, our relationship to self is healthy.

So let's pause here a moment. Go Fish Project is designed for your group to go out into the community and demonstrate the love of Christ.

More than likely, your group will be partnering with and helping those less fortunate than you. Before you go out into the community, I have one request. Think about those you will be helping in terms of the four relationships just mentioned.

God   *Others*

Go Fish Partner

Creation   *Self*

What is your Go Fish partner's relationship status in each of these four areas? Are these relationships dysfunctional? Did the partner make poor choices because he or she didn't have a relationship with God? Was he or she trying to gain fulfillment through others? Has he or she viewed his or her management of God's creation incorrectly? Does the cumulative effect of these relationships distort the partner's view of being one of God's children?

If that is the case, is the partner really any different than you or me? Aren't we all trying to fill a hole that *only* the proper relationship with God can fill? If this isn't aligned, won't this lead us to difficulty in our relationship with others, his creation, and ourselves?

So ... considering today's devotion, what is your relationship status?

Week 2:   Partner

Reflection: Life is experienced through relationships with God and others, and that ultimately affects you.

Scripture: 1 Samuel 24:8–12; 2 Samuel 11:2

> Then David went out of the cave and called out to Saul, "My lord the king!" When Saul looked behind him, David bowed down and prostrated himself with his face to the ground. He said to Saul, "Why do you listen when men say, 'David is bent on harming you'? This day you have seen with your own eyes how the Lord delivered you into my hands in the cave. Some urged me to kill you, but I spared you; I said, 'I will not lay my hand on my lord, because he is the Lord's anointed.' See, my father, look at this piece of your robe in my hand! I cut off the corner of your robe but did not kill you. See that there is nothing in my hand to indicate that I am guilty of wrongdoing or rebellion. I have not wronged you, but you are hunting me down to take my life. May the Lord judge between you and me. And may the Lord avenge the wrongs you have done to me, but my hand will not touch you. (1 Samuel 24:8–12)

> One evening David got up from his bed and walked around on the roof of the palace. From the roof he saw a woman bathing. The woman was very beautiful, and David sent someone to find out about her. (2 Samuel 11:2–3)

Pray/Meditate:

1. We can learn a lot about relationships from David. In the first set of verses, we see that even though Saul was mistreating David, because of Saul's position as God's anointed, David trusted the Lord rather than taking matters into his own hands. His passion for God affected his relationship toward others. And in verse 11 we see that this allowed David to have a clear conscience about himself. However, in the verses from 2 Samuel, when David replaced his passion for God with a passion for Bathsheba, we know the eventual outcome—all the relationships in his life

suffered. Pray for the passion to know God rather than pursuing anything this world can offer.

2. The goal of Go Fish Project is to demonstrate the love of Christ in a world that desperately needs it. Along the way, you will have many chances to reinforce God's design for relationships. Pray that you and your group will demonstrate the love of Christ through your interactions during this project.

3. Next week you will bring a partner into your group. This is a wonderful opportunity to reach out and strengthen a new relationship. Pray for your partner and the new relationship you will create.

5:10 Task: Pick a person in your life who has the relationships mentioned today in perspective. Call, e-mail, or text that person, and thank him or her for his or her witness.

Who's Your Daddy?

What's your name?
Who's your daddy?
Is he rich like me?

Do you recognize that verse from The Zombies 1968 song "Time of the Season"? Funny fact about the song and the group—The Zombies had actually broken up in late 1967 before the song became a hit in America. Even though the group disbanded, the catch phrase "Who's your daddy?" stuck.

In its contemporary form, "Who's your daddy?" has come to represent dominance or power over another. For years, US foreign policy has been one of "Who's your daddy?" We have marched into countries, patrolled the oceans, and secured the skies for the weak, the defenseless, and the oppressed. This foreign policy is often referred to as paternalism, which likens US involvement in world disturbances to a father taking care of his children.

Paternalism is not just confined to US foreign policy. Churches are guilty of this too when we step in to help others when they can actually help themselves. When we swoop in and throw money or a Band-Aid fix to a problem, we leave feeling better about ourselves but often provide only temporary relief. Even worse, we may unintentionally create a dependency on outside help for the locals. As the old saying goes, "Give a man a fish and you feed him for a day; teach a man to fish and you feed him for a lifetime."

Paternalism can occur in three forms when churches seek to help others.[18]

---

18 Steve Corbett and Brian Fikkert. *When Helping Hurts: How to Alleviate Poverty Without Hurting the Poor ... and Yourself.* (Chicago: Moody Publishers, 2009), 110.

- Resource paternalism—pouring financial and other material resources into a problem without including the local people's means in the solution.

- Spiritual paternalism—taking the position that our spiritual experience and knowledge ar somehow deeper than the poor may be presumptuous. Sometimes, in fact, the poor have a deeper walk with God than we do.

- Knowledge paternalism—asserting our solutions on a situation without consulting the locals involved is a mistake. Remember, they know their culture and situation better than we do, so collaborating and listening is always a good idea.

We hope to avoid paternalism in the Go Fish Project by including a partner to listen to and collaborate with during your forty days. As we mentioned yesterday, focusing on relationships during the project forces us to think about the dignity of the individual rather than just completing a task. When we see others through God's eyes, we don't need to ask, "Who's your daddy?" because we already know that we are all his children!

Week Two: Partner

Reflection: Who's your daddy? Are you acting like his child?

Scripture: Galatians 4:6

Because you are his sons, God sent the Spirit of his Son into our hearts, the Spirit who calls out, *"Abba,* Father."

Pray/Meditate:

1. Spend a moment and meditate on the proper context of your relationship with God. He *is* our Daddy. We are his children. Give him the adoration, praise, and honor that he deserves.

2. Reflect on your own inability to reconcile yourself with God. It took his merciful intervention of the cross to redeem his people. Thank God for showing us his grace—and pray that we do the same.

3. Pray for humility as you seek a partner and a project.

5:10 Task: Call, e-mail, or text your pastor and encourage him.

The Homeless Man with the Cardboard Sign

Remember Ted Williams? No, not the famous baseball player, the other one. The homeless guy with the great voice. Who can forget how he skyrocketed to fame when a YouTube video of him displaying his talents went viral overnight? (If you've never seen his story, just search "Ted Williams—Golden Voice" on YouTube)

Ever wonder what happened to him? Back when this happened in 2011, I hoped for the best, but I remember thinking that he would probably use the money to feed his habit of drugs and alcoholism and relapse back into being homeless.

Ted did fall off the wagon briefly, as many do on the road to recovery, but he does seem to have his life back in order. Since being plucked from obscurity, Ted has steady work with Kraft doing voice overs for macaroni and cheese commercials. He recently narrated a documentary.

And he's written a book, appropriately called *A Golden Voice*. He also started the Ted Williams Project—a foundation to give back to those in need.

Here is a quote from Mr. Williams in a recent Fox News report:

> I'm still in recovery. I am looking forward to taking God's message and the message of redemption, hope and of second chances, addiction, mental health and homelessness," Williams added. "The final transition of Ted Williams, the man with the God-given golden voice, I'm ready to spread the message that true redemption is all that he grants. When Christ fed the multitude, he only had five fish and three loaves, and he fed the multitude of people.[19]

---

19   Hollie McKay (contribution by Emily Sissell). "Catching up with Ted "Golden Voice" Williams." http://www.foxnews.com/entertainment/2014/03/14/catching-up-with-ted-golden-voice-williams/. FoxNews.com, posted March 14, 2014.

Given the uphill battle facing Ted and other recovering addicts, I'm not naïve enough to think that there won't be setbacks, but that sounds like a man on the right path. Hopefully the worst mistake he'll make is saying that Christ fed the multitude with *three* loaves, when he actually did it with *two*.

What if I asked you as part of the Go Fish Project, as a way to identify with the poor, to stand on a busy corner in your neighborhood with a cardboard sign that said, "Hungry … will work for food"? Would you do it? Would you be ashamed? Embarrassed? What would happen, heaven forbid, if you actually saw someone you knew?

After thinking about this for a minute, we can brush this hypothetical situation aside, but what if we couldn't? What if we were forced to beg to feed our families? What if we did lose jobs and houses and cars and stuff … and there was nothing left but us?

That, my friend, is the way God views us every day. He sees through the material things we have, just like He saw through the cardboard sign that Ted Williams held. Whether we are materially poor or not makes no difference to our Father. As the Lord said to Samuel the prophet, "Man looks at the outward appearance, but the Lord looks at the heart."

When the Lord looks at your heart, does he see spiritual poverty?

Week 2:   Partner

Reflection: We can be materially wealthy, but spiritually poor.

Scripture: Luke 18:10–14

> "Two men went up to the temple to pray, one a Pharisee and the other a tax collector. The Pharisee stood by himself and prayed: 'God, I thank you that I am not like other people—robbers, evildoers, adulterers—or even like this tax collector. I fast twice a week and give a tenth of all I get.' But the tax collector stood at a distance. He would not even look up to heaven, but beat his breast and said, 'God, have mercy on me, a sinner.' I tell you that this man, rather than the other, went home justified before God. For all those who exalt themselves will be humbled, and those who humble themselves will be exalted."

Pray/Meditate:

1. Spiritual poverty often boils down to the struggle between pride and humility. Jesus railed on the Pharisees' pride throughout the gospels. Notice the actions that the tax collector demonstrated. Pray for the humility of the tax collector.

2. Despite being a spiritual leader, the Pharisee thought God operated on a merit system and that his good works could sway God's opinion. The tax collector, or publican, prayed in a state of repentance and forgiveness. Pray today that the Holy Spirit will reveal areas where you need to repent or to forgive someone.

3. Pray for you and your team to show respect and humility to the Go Fish partner you will choose.

5:10 Task: Go to www.youtubecom and type in "Sidewalk Prophets *Live Like That* official video" and listen to this song about humility.

I Got the Box

Our son Sam has never been one to let grass grow under his feet. Since a very young age, if he decided to do something, consider it done. My wife and I found ourselves scrambling to keep tabs on him during childhood in case his impulsiveness got him into trouble. We covered electrical sockets with safety plugs. We secured our kitchen cabinets with locking clasps. We weren't quite fast enough, however, when at age three he pulled the fire alarm at vacation Bible school. I have never seen that many kids screaming and running out of a building—you would have thought Santa Claus was in the parking lot!

Overall, though, I think we did a pretty good job.

Some of the more benign things he did have made their way into family folklore. One of my favorites is the toy in the cereal box.

My wife, Christy, has always been reasonable when it comes to kids and cereal. She tried to limit the sugary stuff, but occasionally, as a reward or a special treat, she would let them pick the cereal of their choice.

While grocery shopping one day with our three boys, she was feeling benevolent and let them select the cereal they wanted. We aren't totally sure if manipulation was involved or if Sam was just quicker on the draw, but no sooner had my wife made the announcement than Honeycomb was in the shopping cart.

The box of Honeycomb was big and bright yellow, but that is not what caught Sam's six-year-old eyes. It was the promise of the toy figure inside that lured him into the purchase. Given his assertiveness, it took every bit of restraint to make him wait until the next morning to open the box at breakfast.

As you can guess, Sam was first to the table that Saturday morning. Imagine the crushing disappointment when he realized, after thoroughly rummaging through the box, that the toy was not inside!

He brought the box to me and said, "Why can't I get the toy in this box?" I flipped the box over to read the back panel. Just as I feared.

"Sam, I hate to tell you this, but the toy doesn't come in the box." I waited for a response. He just looked at me, so I continued. "To get this toy, you have to prove that you purchased the box. You have to let them know you bought it and then mail them some money to be able to get the action figure."

He understood, but he was hacked. I had seen that look in his eyes before. It made me nervous. Thinking we were finished, I went out into the yard to trim some bushes.

About forty-five minutes later, I noticed Sam marching to the mailbox. He put an envelope inside and went back in the house. I casually moved over to that part of the yard to check what he had done. Given his state of mind, I wanted to make sure there was no anthrax involved.

Instead, what I found brought a smile to my face. On the outside of the envelope he had scribbled, "I got the box." That's it, nothing else. On the inside was a nickel and four pennies.

Sam never wavered from the fact that he wanted the prize—to get it, however, he had to adjust his thinking.

As you go into the preparation phase of the Go Fish Project, I encourage you to adjust your thinking. Rather than approaching your task by asking, "What does this person need?" start with the question, "What gifts and abilities does this person have that can help with this project?" This type of approach to community intervention is called *asset-based community development*, or ABCD. With ABCD, the emphasis is on the person, not the project. Assets are not just monetary either but also the skills, experiences, and capabilities that reside in the person or in the community.

When you take this approach, your Go Fish partner can identify his or her own gifts or abilities or those in the neighborhood that can contribute to improving lives. When you affirm your partner's contribution, you've subtly conveyed the message to your partner: *you are a big part of this project's success.*

Week 2: Partner

Reflection: Poor people have gifts and abilities just like we do, and just like us, God made them to be used.

Scripture: Luke 21:1–4

As Jesus looked up, he saw the rich putting their gifts into the temple treasury. He also saw a poor widow put in two very small copper coins. "Truly I tell you," he said, "this poor widow has put in more than all the others. All these people gave their gifts out of their wealth; but she out of her poverty put in all she had to live on."

Pray/Meditate:

1. Had I been at the temple that day, my instinct would have been to put in money for the poor widow so she could have kept her coins to support herself. To do so, however, would have robbed her of her ability to worship the Lord through giving. Pray that you can identify and bring out your Go Fish partner's gifts and abilities during the project.

2. Pray for the Go Fish partner that will be present at your next team meeting. Pray that he or she will be affirmed during this process and come to see himself or herself as a valuable child of God.

3. Pray for the upcoming team meeting that it will go smoothly as your team and your partner discuss your upcoming project.

5:10 Task: Make a list of the gifts and abilities of your spouse, your children, a friend—someone who is important to you. Share it with that person.

WEEK 3

Week 3—Plan

Team Meeting 3

Step 1   Take a moment and review this week's daily devotions. The emphasis of the week 2 devotions was *the interaction with your Go Fish Project partner.* What did you learn about extending the church out into the community that you may not have realized?

Step 2   The primary goal for the Go Fish Project is to demonstrate the love of Christ. The best way to do that, as Jesus himself said, is to love each other, to build relationships. The actual project you will be doing is secondary.

So before we go on, let's spend a few minutes building relationships. From the ten items below, select *at least* three questions for the team members and partner to answer, allowing time for interaction. If the conversation goes off on a tangent, let it go, but do try to complete at least three questions.

1. What is a personal memory from the 1960s, '70s, '80s, '90s, etc.? (pick as many as you like!)

2. Besides your mom or dad, who is your favorite relative … and why?

3. What is the funniest thing you ever saw happen at *school* or during a *church service*?

4. What is the cheapest date, trip, or vacation that you have ever experienced?

5. What is your favorite sporting event that you attended?

6. Where were you when the September 11 terrorist attack happened? What do you remember about that day? What about these events:

- Elvis on *The Ed Sullivan Show*
- President Kennedy's assassination
- First man on the moon
- Space shuttle *Challenger* explosion
- The first time you got on the Internet
- Your first cell phone

7. If you won the lottery, what would be the first thing you would buy?

8. What is your *favorite* and *least favorite* holiday and why?

9. What kind of work would you do if you didn't have to worry about paying bills? What would be your favorite type of job? Why?

10. If you could sit down and have a conversation with Abraham Lincoln, LeBron James, Lewis and Clark, Oprah, Steve Jobs, or Princess Diana, who would it be? Why?

Step 3   Now we are going to shift gears and start discussing potential projects with your team and your partner. To do this in a collaborative fashion, we are going to approach the project through an asset-based community development system that we discussed last week.

First, share the inventory you created during team meeting 1 with your partner. Point out the variety of gifts, abilities, and resources that the team has, and then discuss the following questions with your partner.

1. The mission of Go Fish Project is to partner with our community to demonstrate the love of Christ. We feel the best way to do that is to hear from those who we will partner with during the project. So naturally, as we start thinking about the project, we want to include you in this process. We believe that God gave every one of us certain gifts and abilities to use, so we want to ask you two questions:

   - What gifts and abilities do you have?
   - What are you good at doing?

This may seem like an odd question, but the reason we ask is that you a lot know more about yourself and your needs than we do. We want to hear from you as we look to partner with you to address any needs or problems.

2. Speaking of needs or problems, is there a specific need or problem that would be helpful if it was addressed by our group?

3. Are there any gifts, abilities, or resources in your neighborhood that could be of help?

4. Is there a way we could use your gifts and abilities and ours in this group to solve the problem together?

Step 4   Put the need or needs discussed in step 3 above in concrete terms. What is the project that needs to be done? What time frame will you need for completion? What tasks need to be organized to complete the project? How will you involve the Go Fish team and the partner in the project? (Use the worksheet located in the appendix.)

Step 5   Pray for the group and the partner to work together to define and address the need identified by the group.

Looking Forward: Appoint at least two people in your group for the following two tasks as we look ahead to team meeting 4 (two people per task):

Task 1: Gather reconnaissance data on your project, and debrief the group on the logistics of the project at your next team meeting. (Include your partner on this task.)

Task 2: Secure and administer the elements for the Lord's Supper, or communion, at the next team meeting. (To prepare for Lord's Supper, see "*Preparation* and *Administration* of Lord's Supper" in the appendix.)

Evel Knievel

Children in the early 1970s had no video games, no cell phones, no iPads, and no laptops. Parents often encouraged us kids to entertain ourselves by playing outdoors. Most of the time it wasn't a suggestion.

Being forced outside with nothing to do really makes you do some crazy stuff, man. We rode bicycles without helmets. We stayed outside all day without putting on sunscreen. We even ate each other's candy without using hand sanitizer.

Nobody was crazier than my brother Kirk, though. He was fascinated with the daredevil Evel Knievel. Knievel made a living out of jumping over things—cars, live sharks, double decker buses, the Grand Canyon—you name it. But the one that caught my brother's attention was his attempt to jump the fountains at Caesar's Palace on ABC's *Wide World of Sports*. The whole neighborhood watched the spectacle but none more closely than my brother. I could see the wheels turning in his head.

Back then, when something cool happened, all the kids met in the alley behind our houses to discuss. Remember, no cell phones. After Evel Knievel's dramatic jump at Caesar's, everyone ran outside to talk about it. My brother, the unofficial ringleader of the neighborhood, started the discussion with, "Man, did you see that?"

"Groovy," came the collective response.

"We can do that!" bragged my brother. Everyone looked at each other. My brother realized his mistake. "No, no, not on a motorcycle—with our bikes!" He was getting more excited the more he talked about it.

The neighborhood kids looked up to Kirk. All ideas from older kids are cool. They were buying it.

At six years old, and the youngest member of our neighborhood gang, it scared me that I was the voice of reason for this group. I tapped my brother on the leg. "What?" he said, irritated that I had interrupted his burgeoning vision.

"Evel Knievel just broke his arms and legs on TV." This fact did not deter my brother. I wish it would have.

He continued. "Okay, how can we make a bicycle jump?" He was using a classic sales move—asking the clients what they thought. Brilliant.

"I've got some cinder blocks," offered Roddy.

"I think we have some plywood for the ramps," said Edward.

"Let's gather up everything and meet back out here in five minutes," said Kirk. "And bring your bikes!"

My mother wouldn't let me jump since I was a novice rider. I was crushed. Had she known the alternative, I think she would have let me ride. You see, the normal ramp-to-ramp jump soon bored my brother. He had just seen Knievel jump over Caesar's Palace fountains—a simple jump just wouldn't do. So they backed up the ramps. Then, to be more like Evel, he began jumping over *things*. First it was a basketball and then our Boston terrier, Brutus. When Brutus (smartly) ran away, my brother looked around for something that would stay put. His eyes locked on me. I ran. I screamed for my mother. Too late.

The neighborhood kids cheered. Mob psychology is sick.

The first jump was a success. After two successful tries, he asked for a second volunteer. My sister ran. She screamed for my mother. Too late. While the mob gathered her in, I was doing the math. One of us would have to be on the end where he landed …

Since you are reading this today, you know that everything turned out fine. My brother made the jump, everyone cheered, and by then it was supper time, so all the kids went home. The thing I still remember to this day is how no one thought jumping humans might not be a good idea. Maybe it was because I had the most at stake that I felt differently.

As you begin to *plan* your Go Fish Project, take the time to hear everyone's opinion—especially the one who has the most at stake—your partner.

Week 3:   Plan

Reflection: None of us are as smart as all of us ...

Scripture: Proverbs 15:22

Plans fail for lack of counsel, but with many advisers they succeed.

Pray/Meditate:

1. Despite being his guinea pig at times, I learned a lot from my brother. He was a great mentor for me in many ways. Take a moment and thank God for childhood and adult friends who encouraged your spiritual development.

2. Reflect on the people in your group. Each has a special, unique gift to bring to this project. Pray that:

    a. Each member will be included in the *plan*

    b. Each member will use his or her gift

3. Pray for your Go Fish Project plan to glorify God and to build each other up.

5:10 Task: Call, text, or e-mail a childhood friend. Reminisce about old times back in the day.

A Quality Individual

On June 24, 1980, NBC television aired the documentary, "If Japan can do it, why can't we?" an in-depth look at the transformation the Japanese automotive and electronics industries made in the years following World War II. The reliability of Japanese designs made startling in-roads in these markets in the 1970s and 1980s—which for years had been dominated by American products.[20]

The documentary placed the industrial transformation that took place in Japan squarely on the shoulders of an obscure PhD in mathematics named W. Edwards Deming. Dr. Deming was an American who made a name for himself constructing the US census in the 1940s. His innovative statistical methods caught the eye of several in the US War Department, so he was sent to Japan under the direction of Douglas McArthur to assist in the rebuilding process following World War II.

Deming's real passion, however, was applying his statistical methods to produce quality products. A recovering Japan was the perfect lab for his experiment. Deming spent extensive time in Japan during the 1950s and 1960s, consulting on extended visits seven different times. Upon his departure, the Japanese auto industry had adapted his techniques of production and management.

After the documentary aired on NBC, Deming's phone began to ring. Suddenly, this little-known statistician was in demand. Everyone realized his strengths and the value he could bring to their companies. So at eighty years old, he went to work for Ford Motor Company. And you know what? He turned them around too.

---

20   Agis Salpukas, "U.S. Car Sales at 19-year Low." Article in the *New York Times*, printed January 8, 1981. Accessed at: http://www.nytimes.com/1981/01/08/business/1980-car-sales-at-19-year-low.html on July 21, 2014.

Seven years later, in 1987, President Ronald Reagan awarded the National Medal of Technology to Deming. Reagan also established the Malcolm Baldridge Quality Award, named after the president's secretary of commerce. The award was based on much of the philosophy of Deming.[21]

I did not know Dr. Deming, but I can imagine the joy he must have felt when someone in his own country finally asked him about his ideas. This was a man who spent considerable time writing, lecturing, and teaching his methods to an overseas audience. What it must have done for his self-esteem even at eighty years old!

As you plan your Go Fish Project, think about Dr. Deming—not necessarily how to apply his statistical methods to your project but rather how to include everyone in it. Your team and your partner have unique gifts and skills placed in them by our Lord to be used for just such an occasion. Add to their joy by utilizing those gifts.

21   The W. Edwards Deming Institute, accessed at: https://www.deming.org/theman/timeline, on July 21, 2014.

Week 3:	Plan
Reflection:	Use your gifts for God's glory.
Scripture:	1 Kings 7:13–14

King Solomon sent to Tyre and brought Huram, whose mother was a widow from the tribe of Naphtali and whose father was from Tyre and a skilled craftsman in bronze. Huram was filled with wisdom, with understanding and with knowledge to do all kinds of bronze work. He came to King Solomon and did all the work assigned to him.

Pray/Meditate:

1. Take a moment and humble yourself before God. Speak to his greatness, and acknowledge your limitations. Then ask the Almighty to show you the gifts he gave you. This should be an extremely personal interaction between you and God. Do not shy away from it—he knows you better than anyone.

2. Next, ask him how you can best use your gifts for his glory. Take time to listen to what He has to say.

3. No other worker is mentioned by name in the scriptural account of the construction of King Solomon's temple. Huram was known for his craftsmanship. Pray that each person on your team will have a chance to demonstrate his or her skill during the project to the glory of God.

5:10 Task:	Include a friend, a family member, or a coworker in a decision. Ask for his or her opinion.

Feeling God's Pleasure ...

Track star Eric Liddell is considered to be Scotland's greatest Olympic hero. With head tilted straight back, mouth wide open, and arms clawing at the air, his running style might have been a little bit unorthodox compared to today's fluid speedsters. But, oh—he could run.

The 1981 movie classic *Chariots of Fire* introduced many to Liddell and his running style for the first time. But moviegoers didn't leave the film talking about his odd running technique; they left talking about his integrity.

Liddell was the odds-on favorite to win multiple races in the 1924 Paris Olympics. As a sprinter, Eric's best races were the hundred-meter and two hundred–meter dashes. But he refused to run in the hundred-meter race because the preliminary heats were scheduled for Sunday—the Sabbath day, and a day of rest.

In the movie version, the decision to run or not is portrayed as a last-second decision that Liddell struggled with internally; in actuality, he made his decision months before the Olympics once he saw the schedule. Some might wonder, would Eric Liddell do the same thing today if he was participating in the Olympics? Could he forego the fame and the fortune that comes with being an Olympic medalist? Liddell was once asked whether giving up international athletics bothered him. "It's natural for a chap to think over all that sometimes but I'm glad I'm at the work I'm engaged in now," Liddell said. "A fellow's life counts for far more at this than the other."[22]

The "this" he was referring to was his missionary work. The son of Chinese missionaries, Liddell was born in China in 1902 and died there

---

22   Simon Burnton, *The Guardian*. "50 stunning Olympic moments: No8 Eric Liddell's 400 metres win, 1924". January 2012.

in 1945. Soon after the Paris Olympics, Liddell became a missionary there himself, where he would serve for the remainder his life.

He spent twenty years teaching children English in one of the poorest areas in China—a region torn apart by years of civil war. During World War II, the territory was also prone to altercations from the neighboring Japanese. Fearing for the safety of his family, he sent his pregnant wife home with their two other girls in the early 1940s. His fears were realized as he was taken as prisoner of war in 1943. Liddell died in the prisoner of war camp just five months before liberation.

To honor him before the 2008 Olympics in Shanghai, Chinese officials disclosed to the Liddell family that Winston Churchill made arrangements with the Japanese government for a prisoner swap at the camp involving Liddell. True to his character, he sent a pregnant woman in his place. Langdon Gilkey, who was a companion of Liddell's in the prisoner of war camp and future prominent theologian, said, "It is rare indeed that a person has the good fortune to meet a saint, but he came as close to it as anyone I have ever known."[23]

A track masseur at the Paris Olympics must have thought the same thing. As Liddell kneeled at the starting blocks of his four hundred–meter race, the masseur slipped him a note scribbled with the words from 1 Samuel 2:30: "Those who honor me, I will honor."

Eric Liddell honored God by living a life of integrity. In *Chariots of Fire*, when his sister Jennie questioned that integrity, Liddell said, "I believe God made me for a purpose. For China. But he also made me fast. And when I run, I feel his pleasure. To give it up would be to hold him in contempt."

For what purpose did God make you? As you plan the Go Fish Project, contribute—and feel God's pleasure!

---

23   Ibid.

Week 3:	Plan
Reflection:	To feel God's pleasure, don't stand on the sidelines—get in the race!
Scripture:	1 Corinthians 9:24–27

Do you not know that in a race all the runners run, but only one gets the prize? Run in such a way as to get the prize. Everyone who competes in the games goes into strict training. They do it to get a crown that will not last, but we do it to get a crown that will last forever. Therefore I do not run like someone running aimlessly; I do not fight like a boxer beating the air. [27] No, I strike a blow to my body and make it my slave so that after I have preached to others, I myself will not be disqualified for the prize.

Pray/Meditate:

1. As you pray today, ask God to look in the corners of your life where we sometimes miss when we sweep. Like the rich young ruler, ask him for direction toward the straight and narrow path. (FYI, he already knows what you need, but he likes it when you ask!)

2. Nothing hurts the Christian movement more than hypocrisy. People like Eric Liddell remind us that there is no gray area when it comes to integrity. He honored God with his living sacrifice. Pray that you and your team will run the race and complete your project in a way that pleases and honors our Lord.

3. Pray for the household and/or the community where your project will be located.

| **5:10 Task:** | Search www.youtube.com for the *Chariots of Fire* movie trailer and watch it! |

Dreams and Dry Heaves

We have already introduced you to our son Sam in devotional 14. In second grade, Sam contracted Crohn's disease. Because of the severity of the symptoms, he was prescribed total parenteral nutrition (TPN) for a few months by his physician. TPN is a form of nutritional therapy that bypasses the digestive system completely by providing calories intravenously via a central line.

Despite the fact that I was the parent with a medical background, my wife took on the responsibility of hooking up Sam to the machine each evening and breaking it down the next morning ... as long as she didn't have to look at the central line in his arm. She is a self-proclaimed wimp when it comes to anything medical. She cannot handle anything involving blood, needles, and/or pain. I can assure you she got nauseous just reading the previous sentence.

So our normal routine was that Sam and I checked out the central line port each morning and each evening to make sure it was clean, dry, and free from infection. We would carefully wrap it back so only the end was protruding so Christy could take over and hook the machine up to pump through the night.

Sam slept on a couch in our bedroom during that time in case the IV went beep in the night—as they are prone to do. After about a week, we had worked out all the bugs and had it down to a science.

One night, however, we had a bit of a hiccup.

I was in deep REM sleep when the person I was looking at in my dream said, "Dad, I'm bleeding everywhere." I was hovering between being conscious and yet still dreaming. The voice repeated, "Dad, are you awake? I'm bleeding." I was coming to but still very confused. The IV wasn't beeping and Sam wasn't screaming in pain, so none of this made sense. I fumbled for my glasses but picked up Sam's by mistake. The little arms weren't long enough to fit over my earlobes. I was too groggy to realize that they weren't mine, so I just stuck them into my ear canal so they would stay put.

I turned on a bedside lamp, but that just made matters worse. Sam's prescription was for near-sightedness; mine was for far-sightedness. Sam looked like he was in the next room. I assessed the situation the best I could. Sam was soaking wet. There was fluid everywhere—the sheets, the couch, the floor—but it wasn't blood.

I gathered myself together enough to comprehend the gravity of the situation. The IV was pumping out the bag of fluids, but that meant the central line must be compromised. A central line infection is serious business. I asked Sam to check his port site for damage while I switched glasses. He unwrapped the soggy ace bandage on his arm and cheerfully reported, "Nope. Look. Still perfect." He gave the catheter a little tug to show it was still intact.

By now, Christy had joined the party, but she was where I was a few minutes earlier—still mentally confounded. She looked at Sam just as he was yanking at the central line. She disappeared into the shadows of our bedroom.

I looked at Sam's arm in the light. "Hey, Dad, look," Sam said—a big grin on his face. He pointed across the room. Christy was on her hands and knees dry heaving. While we waited for mom, Sam and I located the problem—an IV line clasp that controlled the flow of nutrients was missing—and guess who had to fix it? The lady in the corner on all fours.

I cleaned the area while Sam rewrapped his arm with a new, dry ace bandage. Christy gathered herself and her supplies together, and in no time the team had Sam back up and running.

"I am proud of you, Sam," I said after it was all over.

"Me too," said Mom.

Sam smiled mischievously. He looked at Christy and said, "It was funny when I pulled at the tube in my arm and ..." But she didn't hear the rest—she was back in the corner on all fours.

Week 3:   Plan

Reflection: Teams are always stronger than individuals

Scripture: Ecclesiastes 4:9–10, 12; 1 Corinthians 1:10

> Two are better than one, because they have a good return for their labor: If either of them falls down, one can help the other up But pity anyone who falls and has no one to help them up ... Though one may be overpowered, two can defend themselves. A cord of three strands is not quickly broken. (Ecclesiastes 4:9–10, 12)

> I appeal to you, brothers and sisters, in the name of our Lord Jesus Christ, that all of you agree with one another in what you say and that there be no divisions among you, but that you be perfectly united in mind and thought. (1 Corinthians 1:10)

Pray/Meditate:

1. Spend a moment and ask the Lord to reveal how his church is supposed to function. Pray for forgiveness where the church has squabbled over petty issues while the world suffers. Pray that his church around the world will unite together to show the love of Christ.

2. Pray for the spiritual healing of our nation.

3. Pray for your group to be united as you go out into the community.

5:10 Task: Call, text, or e-mail someone who supported you during a difficult time.

Bifocals

Up until the age of sixteen, I wore bifocals. Let that sink in a minute. Sixteen with bifocals. Oh yeah, and they were black, horn-rimmed. I am not making this up. How I have any self-esteem today is a testament to my sense of humor and thick skin. I actually thought people were laughing *with* me.

During childhood, I don't remember being bullied about my bifocals. Perhaps it was because I was proactive. I used creative measures to make my eyewear appear cool to my friends. For instance, I would let them borrow my glasses to burn fire ants. Or a real crowd favorite was passing them around during class. If you held the bifocals just right, with the line between the lenses dividing the teacher in half, her top half was tall and skinny and her bottom half was short and fat, making her look like a talking pear. Math was never so fun!

By adolescence, though, I had had enough. Do you know how it feels to have your parents ask for your glasses so they can read the menu in restaurants? It made my parents look cheap and well, to be honest, pathetic. By this point, I had decided. My driver's license picture was not going to look like Roy Orbison.

The plan was to get contacts for my sixteenth birthday, so I pestered my mom relentlessly in the months leading up to the big day. She resisted until I played hardball on the menu reading. She set up the appointment with my ophthalmologist the next day.

On the day of the appointment, I was anxious. The nurse took me back and dilated my eyes. I practiced my speech over and over. Finally, the doctor entered the exam room. Showtime. I slowly lowered the flimsy sunglasses as maturely as I could. It was time to discuss, man to man, a simple business transaction. So he would understand my conviction on the matter, I looked him straight in the eyes. However, the examination light behind him seared my dilated retinas, causing me to tear up. The doctor was touched by this perceived emotion. He agreed to my demands. It was time to try contacts! Wait. What? I didn't even get a chance to finish my speech.

I was so happy I blew right past the conditions ...

In order to get contacts, I had to wean myself off bifocals first. I had to train my eyes from looking through two lenses down to one. My doctor said I needed to do this for twelve weeks. No big deal I thought—twelve weeks to freedom!

He presented two options.

Option 1 was costly. My parents would have to fork over $250 for a new pair of glasses that I would only wear for twelve weeks. I knew this would never work. My dad was an accountant. Other accountants called him thrifty behind his back. He routinely required us kids to look for pennies every time we went to the mall. Because of my bifocals, loose change was magnified on the ground. Compared to my siblings, my productivity was through the roof. There was no way he was going to lose me as a revenue stream. Option 1 was off the table before we left the office.

Option 2 was costly also, but not in a monetary sense. Realizing my dad's desire for the cheap route, my doctor quickly whipped out a roll of scotch tape and an X-Acto knife. He covered the bottom half of my glasses with the scotch tape, and with his skilled surgical hands, he trimmed the edges. In sixty seconds he occluded the bottom lens, and *voila*! I had my single-lens glasses.

He stood back and grinned. My father grinned. My siblings laughed. My mother looked away. One roll of $1.29 scotch tape would last the necessary twelve weeks. Shoot, I could find $1.29 with one pass in the food court on the way home. Sold!

An hour before when I walked into the doctor's office, thanks to years of wearing bifocals, my self-dignity and pride hung on by a thread. When I walked out, I had neither. Option 2 took care of that. I would be forced to wear the taped-up glasses at school for twelve weeks. Please don't forget that I was sixteen. It really wasn't when I was going to get beat up, it was how often.

I prepared for the worst. I drew up a will. I left my eyes to science so that somehow, some way, some smart researcher wearing bifocals could prevent this from happening to another kid.

Over the weekend I perfected my tape-application technique so that the edges of the tape blended into the frames beautifully. I actually thought they looked pretty good. At school I went on the offensive. I asked everyone what they thought of my new "smoky-lens" glasses. I bragged that it was in vogue in the larger cities. I noted that Robin Leach sported a pair himself on *Lifestyles of the Rich and Famous*. And you know what? They bought it.

Twelve weeks later, I went to school touting my new Bausch & Lomb breathable contact lenses.

I loved the idea of contact lenses, but I had to sacrifice to get them.

Jesus loved the idea of having a relationship with all people, but he had to sacrifice to get them. Can't we sacrifice a little to help him?

Week 3:	Plan
Reflection:	Nothing worth achieving comes without sacrifice.
Scripture:	Jeremiah 29:11; Isaiah 30:19–21

For I know the plans I have for you," declares the Lord, "plans to prosper you and not to harm you, plans to give you hope and a future. (Jeremiah 29:11)

People of Zion, who live in Jerusalem, you will weep no more. How gracious he will be when you cry for help! As soon as he hears, he will answer you. Although the Lord gives you the bread of adversity and the water of affliction, your teachers will be hidden no more; with your own eyes you will see them. Whether you turn to the right or to the left, your ears will hear a voice behind you, saying, "This is the way; walk in it." (Isaiah 30:19–21)

Pray/Meditate:

1. As you plan your Go Fish Project, know that God may require you to sacrifice your time, talents, and resources. In doing so, you become like Christ, who sacrificed all to redeem his people. Thank God for the privilege of continuing Christ's mission of compassion.

2. It is a beautiful thing when the plans of the people fulfill the plans of God. Pray that your Go Fish Project plan will accomplish exactly what God desires for you, your team, and your partner.

3. Finally, pray that the Holy Spirit clarifies what the eventual plan will be for your group.

5:10 Task: Call, text, or e-mail someone who has sacrificed something for you—a parent, your spouse, a friend, or a boss—and thank him or her.

Snow Cones and School Records

My oldest son, Britton, has a personality that often leaves him conflicted. His extremely competitive nature is balanced by a tender heart for people. In most individuals, one of these traits will be preferred more than the other.

We knew Britton was a perfect blend of both traits during his second-grade year. At the elementary school he attended, one PE teacher encouraged students to enter the annual running competition. On certain days the kids could run once their normal activities were finished, and the teacher would record their mileage and keep track of it over the course of the school year. Like any competition, the first semester started with a large group clustered together. With the colder weather over winter, a smaller pack separated itself from the rest of the second grade. At the head of that pack were two students—our son Britton and a cute little girl named Kaitlyn.

By the time spring break rolled around, these two had far out distanced the others. They had accumulated well over 120 miles for the year and were neck and neck heading into the final week of school. As parents, Christy and I encouraged Britton to stick with it and see if he could set the elementary school record, which was well within reach.

During that final week, I was secretly hoping Kaitlyn would sprain an ankle or come down with a mild case of bronchitis—something with a quick recovery but that would keep her from running and assure Britton of the school record. Much to my chagrin, however, Kaitlyn pulled slightly ahead of Britton in those last few days. I had given up any hope of victory.

We didn't give it another thought until the end-of-the-year awards assembly. During the PE portion of the program, the teacher who sponsored the competition took a moment to recognize the students for running over the entire school year.

"But," she said, "I want to specifically point out two special students who competed all year and ended up in a tie with one hundred and twenty-nine miles a piece! They both set a new school record in the process." What? Something must have happened during the final week. I noticed that when she gave Kaitlyn and Britton the award, she hugged Britton a little longer.

I was pumped. Britton must have smoked Kaitlyn that last day! That's my boy! Afterward the PE teacher made a beeline for us in the crowd. I was ready to receive the accolades about Britton's competitive fire. Instead, with tears in her eyes, she said, "Do you know what this young gentleman did?"

I smiled. I thought I heard *Chariots of Fire* playing faintly in the background. She went on. "Britton could have set the school record by himself this year. But since Kaitlyn wasn't at school the last day of running, he just stopped when he knew that he had tied her. He wanted both of them to win."

The tender heart side of his personality obviously came from his mother, not me.

Apparently once the record was secured, Britton was satisfied. He felt a snow cone was in order, so he just pulled over and ordered one at the school canteen. He wasn't conflicted at all. He came in first and made a friend in the process.

Week 3:	Plan
Reflection:	Plan your Go Fish Project, but allow for flexibility.
Scripture:	Acts 19:8–12

Paul entered the synagogue and spoke boldly there for three months, arguing persuasively about the kingdom of God. But some of them became obstinate; they refused to believe and publicly maligned the Way. So Paul left them. He took the disciples with him and had discussions daily in the lecture hall of Tyrannus. This went on for two years, so that all the Jews and Greeks who lived in the province of Asia heard the word of the Lord. God did extraordinary miracles through Paul, so that even handkerchiefs and aprons that had touched him were taken to the sick, and their illnesses were cured and the evil spirits left them.

Pray/Meditate:

1. Britton had a plan for the running competition—it just wasn't mine. And it was actually better. God uses people in ways that we cannot fully appreciate on this side of heaven. Allow him room as you plan. Pray for discernment to follow the Holy Spirit as your project unfolds.

2. Paul was on his third missionary journey when these verses took place. Look at verse 10 closely. Because of his willingness to obey the Lord, all the Jews and Greeks heard the word of the Lord. Pray for the willingness to obey the commands of our Lord.

3. The result of Paul's flexibility and obedience? All of Asia heard the good news, and God did extraordinary miracles through Paul. What could God do today if we did the same? Reflect for a moment, and ask God to show you what the united church can do by obeying his commands. Without obedience, the *united* church becomes *untied*.

5:10 Task: Treat a friend to coffee, tea, or a snow cone!

E Pluribus Unum

Translation: From many, one

It was the summer of 1977. My brother had just graduated from high school, and my mother wanted to combine a celebratory graduation gift with our family vacation. We rarely took extended family vacations like this one, so Mom had a laundry list of chores to do before she felt comfortable leaving. I didn't care. All I knew was that I was ten years old and we were going to Disney World. Looking back as a parent now, I can appreciate the effort it took to prepare for the trip. Back then, I just realized that my mom had kicked it up a notch. Space Mountain? Not even on the radar yet. Hall of Presidents? She vetoed any talk of that. The Jungle Cruise? We would miss that port of call unless we all worked together to prepare for the trip.

I can still remember the vacation planning session around the table on Sunday night after church. Six days until Florida. "Eat your corned beef and hash," she said. "I heard there was a new Bonanza restaurant in Kissimmee, and I want to splurge and eat there one night." Wow, Bonanza! I pictured myself in a booth looking up at the wagon-wheel chandeliers—my mom was a masterful motivator.

For the next thirty minutes, she assigned tasks for the family to come together and complete before we left town. Sibling rivalry became sibling resolve. There was yard work, car servicing, mail stoppage, room cleaning, pet grooming, and suitcase packing. As oppressive as that might have sounded to a ten-year-old, I loved that week leading up to our Disney trip. Nobody complained about their assignments. Nobody cared about who got credit for doing what. We all pitched in to make sure everything was finished.

Throughout the week of preparation, my mom sprinkled in tales of adventure that awaited us in Florida. There were glass-bottom boats in Silver Springs; panoramic views of orange groves from the Citrus Tower in Orlando; and of course, the pinnacle of the trip itself—the Magic Kingdom! We worked together, dare I say, joyfully, knowing what was at the end of our labor. We even saw the usually businesslike exchanges between our parents soften with smiles and laughter during that week.

One family, one mission—all working together. Nothing made my mom happier than to watch her family come together and act as one. You can rest assured Jesus feels the same.

Week 3:   Plan

Reflection: Imagine if Christians around the globe united as one to extend Christ's love into the world …

Scripture: Ephesians 4:4–6

> There is *one* body and
> > *one* Spirit—just as you were called to
> > *one* hope when you were called—
> > *one* Lord,
> > *one* faith,
> > *one* baptism;
> *one* God and Father of all, who is over all and through all and in all.

Pray/Meditate:

For the early church in Ephesus, Paul urged *one* plus *one* plus *one* plus *one* plus *one* plus *one* plus *one* equals *one*. The math may not be good, but the strategy is flawless. There is strength in unity.

1. Pray for the Holy Spirit to reveal areas in your life where demonstrating unity is important—relationships, family, work, etc.

2. Pray for your group to go out into your community with singleness of purpose—to demonstrate the love of Christ.

3. Pray for churches everywhere to practice *e pluribus unum*—from many, one.

5:10 Task: Pull together your family, and vote on your favorite family vacation!

WEEK 4

Week 4—Perform

Team Meeting 4

Step 1   Take a moment and review the past week's daily devotions. The emphasis for the week 3 devotions was *planning the Go Fish Project with your partner.* How does knowing that God created each of us with gifts and abilities to bring glory to him change your thoughts about yourself and others? How will you look at your gifts and those of others a little differently now?

Step 2   The next phase of Go Fish Project is to perform your identified project with your partner. Before your group goes out, however, allow the group members who did the reconnaissance to report back to the group.

Step 3   Based on this report, does your group need to tweak the initial plans you made during last week's team meeting? If so, make sure everyone understands the game plan so each member is on the same page. Once finished with this discussion, your group is ready to go out into the community!

Step 4   As your group prepares to enter into the community, it is good idea to partake of the Lord's Supper. Jesus taught his disciples that the Supper was a symbol of his new covenant of redemption and grace. He knew that they would draw strength in the future as they looked back on this intimate and deeply personal dinner. (Refer to the appendix for administration.)

Step 5   Close the meeting in prayer; specifically, pray for:

- the work to be a blessing;

- the work to build relationships between the team, the partner, the community, and our Lord;

- the safety of all participants;

- the completion of the work; and

- the name of our Lord to be glorified through our efforts.

Looking forward, team meeting 5 in a couple of weeks will be less of a meeting and more of a celebration for the project's completion. Take a few minutes and plan the details of the celebration. What do you want it to be? Lunch? Dinner? At a home? At a restaurant? Schedule the date to coincide with the end of the forty days if you can. Now ... go get to work on your project!

Above My Pay Grade

On August 17, 2008, as the United States readied for the upcoming presidential election, Pastor Rick Warren moderated the Saddleback Civil Forum on the Presidency. Warren asked candidates Barak Obama and John McCain a series of specific questions designed to elicit their positions on a variety of important world views.

Below is an excerpt from that night. The question specifically dealt with the topic of abortion, and Mr. Obama's response included a phrase that has made it into our vernacular since then:

> *Warren*: As a pastor, I have to deal with this all of the time, all of the pain and all of the conflicts. I know this is a very complex issue. Forty million abortions, at what point does a baby get human rights, in your view?

> *Obama*: Well, you know, I think that whether you're looking at it from a theological perspective or a scientific perspective, answering that question with specificity, you know, is *above my pay grade.*[24]

Perhaps this was an artful dodge of the question by our future president, but his answer was more truthful than he knew. Only the Lord God Almighty has all the right answers. Jesus said it himself in John 14:6: "I am the way, the truth, and the life."

I am convinced that we as Christians need to spend more time above our pay grade in order to understand what we truly are up against. Allow me to illustrate.

---

24   Saddleback Presidential Candidates Forum—Transcript; Accessed at: http://transcripts.cnn.com/TRANSCRIPTS/0808/16/se.02.html. Program originally aired on August 16, 2008. Accessed July 26, 2014.

As a business leadership consultant, I am amazed at the disconnect that often exists between executive leaders in a company and their front-line staff. Both groups typically function in their own worlds, intersecting only when circumstances make it necessary. As a result, employees are less engaged and view work basically as a means to a paycheck.

However, keen CEOs who reach out to employees know that they can provide a fresh perspective of the organization to the workforce. Two critical things happen when CEOs interact with lower ranks in the organization:

1. The employees walk away with a better understanding of the bigger picture. A simple explanation of why executive leadership in their company is pursuing a particular course can build trust that permeates the culture.

2. Employees understand how their individual jobs impact the overall health of the organization. When that happens, employee engagement, and thus, productivity, goes through the roof.

So let's put this in the context of Christianity. Our Lord and CEO, chief evangelistic officer, spent time among us in the form of Jesus Christ. He reached out to us and gave us the mission of his organization, the church:

> Therefore go and make disciples of all nations, baptizing them in the name of the Father and of the Son and of the Holy Spirit, and teaching them to obey everything I have commanded you.[25]

He also promised to listen to us in the form of prayer—anytime we ask:

> If my people, who are called by my name, will humble themselves and pray and seek my face and turn from their wicked ways, then I will hear from heaven, and I will forgive their sin and will heal their land.[26]

So, if our Lord has extended the offer to interact with us, why are we not more engaged as his employees? The answer is simple—we haven't spent enough time above our pay grade. The more we listen to him in prayer,

---

25   Matthew 28:19–20
26   2 Chronicles 7:14

then we see the bigger picture, and the more we want to be obedient. We see things from his perspective and not from our isolated, simple one. We see that we are employed to fight in a very real battle of good versus evil.

As you perform your Go Fish Project, know that you are being obedient to the one above your pay grade!

Week 4:   Perform

Reflection: We are in a spiritual battle of good versus evil.

Scripture: 2 Corinthians 10:3–5

> For though we live in the world, we do not wage war as the world does. The weapons we fight with are not the weapons of the world. On the contrary, they have divine power to demolish strongholds. We demolish arguments and every pretension that sets itself up against the knowledge of God, and we take captive every thought to make it obedient to Christ.

Pray/Meditate:

1. Reflect for a moment about the God who is above your pay grade. Spend time acknowledging his power, his authority, his holiness, and his sovereignty.

2. Pray for the Holy Spirit to give you fresh insight into the battle of good versus evil that is ongoing all around us. Ask for examples that reveal this battle to you.

3. Pray that you and your team are faithful employees in the work against evil.

5:10 Task: Jot down three things that you would consider evil in the world today. It could be a person, a practice, or a problem. Then write down, "Divine power to demolish stronghold" out beside each item. Spend time with God praying that evil is destroyed, all to his glory.

Week 4—Perform

The Only Thing We Have to Fear ...

Franklin Roosevelt won the 1932 presidential election, beating Herbert Hoover by a landslide. America was in the depth of the Great Depression, and President Roosevelt ran on a platform that promised the public that better days were ahead. From that 1932 inaugural address came the most famous quote from his twelve years as president:

> So, first of all, let me assert my firm belief that the only thing we have to fear is fear itself—nameless, unreasoning, unjustified terror which paralyzes needed efforts to convert retreat into advance.[27]

President Roosevelt's words were meant to inspire and encourage Americans during a dark time in our history. Those same words could apply to Christians today.

Let's be honest. It is a dark time in our history again. The Christian America that answered Roosevelt's call eighty-two years ago is vastly different than the one we know. American today cannot be described as Christian. But rather than pointing fingers at who dropped the ball or assign fault to a group or party, let's use today's devotion to strengthen our resolve.

Remember how many times we are told not to fear in the Bible. Fear paralyzes. It produces worry and anxiety over things that never happen. More than anything, fear weakens our faith. The Lord knows that faith and fear cannot coexist in the heart of a believer.

During the Great Depression, people and businesses hunkered down in hopes of simply weathering the storm. Roosevelt urged Americans

---

27   National Archives Identifier: 197333. File Unit : First Carbon Files, 1933 - 1945, Collection FDR-PPF: Papers as President, President's Personal File, 1933 - 1945.

to convert retreat into action. As president and leader of our nation, Roosevelt was unwavering in his faith that the might of the American people would restore our good fortune. Slowly, the nation and the people responded. By the time World War II was forced upon us with the bombing of Pearl Harbor, fear was never mentioned. We were resolute in our action.

We can learn from President Roosevelt's example of faith over fear. He put Benjamin Franklin's words into practice: "The man who achieves makes many mistakes, but he never makes the biggest mistake of all—doing nothing."[28]

President Roosevelt guided a mighty nation at one of her weakest points. As Christians, we are also a mighty nation at one of our weakest points. But we don't have a frail, human president as our leader; we have none other than Jesus—the Alpha and Omega, the Firstborn over all Creation, the King of Kings and Lord of Lords. Will we hunker down in fear and just wait for Christ's return, or will we go out in faith? I think it's time to turn retreat into action. After all, what do we have to fear?

---

28 Ben Franklin: https://sites.google.com/site/kondabhaskarreddy/benjamin-franklin-pennsylvania-gazette

Week 4:   Perform

Reflection: As you go, go in faith.

Scripture: Isaiah 41:9–13

"I took you from the ends of the earth, from its farthest corners I called you. I said, 'You are my servant'; I have chosen you and have not rejected you. So do not fear, for I am with you; do not be dismayed, for I am your God. I will strengthen you and help you; I will uphold you with my righteous right hand. All who rage against you will surely be ashamed and disgraced; those who oppose you will be as nothing and perish. Though you search for your enemies, you will not find them. Those who wage war against you will be as nothing at all. For I am the Lord your God who takes hold of your right hand and says to you, 'Do not fear; I will help you.'"

Pray/Meditate:

1. For a moment, fear God. Fear his judgment. Fear being separated from him eternally. Fear his holiness next to your sin. Fear not obeying his perfect commands. Fear a world without him.

2. Now, spend a few minutes in God's presence *fearing nothing*! Whatever you fear, whatever worries you, whatever takes your eyes off him, strengthen your faith by laying it all at his feet right now.

3. Pray for faith over fear as you perform your Go Fish Project.

5:10 Task: Face a fear today. Do something that you have been dreading. Don't avoid it any longer!

<u>Seventy-Nine Days</u>

In 1975 Pepsi launched a brilliant marketing campaign called the Pepsi Challenge. If you are over forty years old, I'm sure you remember the commercials vividly.

An unsuspecting volunteer, usually in malls, in a park, or on the street, was asked to take a sip from two cups marked A and B sitting on a table. While the audience watched the surprised participants pick Pepsi time and time again, an announcer described how people chose Pepsi over Coke in nationwide taste tests.

After a few years, the Coca-Cola Company had had enough. The Pepsi Challenge and the tagline, "The choice of a new generation" threatened to erode the long-standing grip Coke held on the soft drink industry.

So on April 23, 1985, Coca-Cola introduced a new formula to compete with the sweeter taste identified by the Pepsi Challenge as the choice people preferred. The public response was swift and unexpected—people hated the new Coke. I was one of those people.

Coca-Cola executives had anticipated the pushback upon entry into the market, but their own secret taste tests had in fact confirmed that people did favor the sweeter formula. They justified their actions, assuming the public response would subside and once again Coca-Cola would reign supreme. But the backlash against the new Coke worsened. People snatched all the old coke off grocery shelves. Atlanta hadn't been so mad since Sherman marched through on his way to the sea.

So on July 11, 1985, Coca-Cola executives reintroduced the original formula and named it Coca-Cola classic. New Coke fizzed out after only seventy-nine days. Was it all just a brilliant marketing move by Coke? Did they know all along that they were going to remove the original Coke for a while, only to remarket it to an adoring public?

We may never know the reason, but the take-home message is this: Coca-Cola listened to the consumer and acted. They had seen enough of Pepsi eating into their share of soft drinks, so they did something. They protected their brand.

If you are listening to what people are saying about the church, we are increasingly being portrayed as an ancient, irrelevant relic to society. It's time to act. Let's show the world we are still significant. And I think we can do it in forty days instead of seventy-nine!

Week 4:	Perform
Reflection:	Go! Make a difference!
Scripture:	James 2:14–20

What good is it, my brothers and sisters, if someone claims to have faith but has no deeds? Can such faith save them? Suppose a brother or a sister is without clothes and daily food. If one of you says to them, "Go in peace; keep warm and well fed," but does nothing about their physical needs, what good is it? In the same way, faith by itself, if it is not accompanied by action, is dead. But someone will say, "You have faith; I have deeds." Show me your faith without deeds, and I will show you my faith by my deeds. You believe that there is one God. Good! Even the demons believe that—and shudder. You foolish person, do you want evidence that faith without deeds is useless?

Pray/Meditate:

1. As you go out to do your Go Fish Project, pray for your team, your partner, and your community.

2. Pray that the actions of your team will bring glory to God.

3. Pray for the global church to become socially relevant again and to heal the world of its problems through the power of our Lord.

5:10 Task: Go to www.youtube.com and type "New Coke 1985" and relive some memories …

Jesus Had a Green Thumb

Plants have a relatively short life at our house. While we enjoy the color and warmth plants bring to a home, any foliage at our house better be hearty to survive. The simple reason is that my wife and I are not good with details. The regular schedule of watering, pruning, and nurturing just does not register with us. Now that our children are old enough to understand this about us, they consider themselves fortunate to have survived their upbringing.

Imagine our surprise, then, when my wife's best friends, Genie and Traci, gave her two satsuma trees one year for her birthday. The gift was thoughtful. Their intentions were noble. We had a child who was on a special diet at the time, and satsumas hit the jackpot—they were on the diet, and our son loved them. But surely they knew of the impending death sentence they just gave those poor fruit trees. Of all people, Genie and Traci understood that this was a lady who makes to-do lists and then forgets where she put them.

However, we thanked them profusely for such a meaningful gift. Later that day I dutifully planted them. We watered them pretty well at first. My wife and I wanted to at least give the appearance that we expected them to live, but we didn't hold much hope. Sure enough, we missed a day of watering due to a basketball game, and from that point on, the weak little satsuma trees were on their own.

Strange thing, though, they grew. Despite our forgetfulness, they grew. Forgot to water them. Never fertilized them. Never cut them back. They just grew. And guess what? Those trees did what they were planted for despite no encouragement or help from us—they produced fruit.

Shouldn't we as Christians do the same? I find myself longing for the perfect environment so I can one day produce spiritual fruit. The kids grown. Work less stressful. Finances under control. I have mistakenly created this mythical spiritual greenhouse, where the climate is perfect, the soil is moist, and the sun always shines. When those elements all come together, then I can produce fruit. By doing so, I limit what the Gardener can do through me.

Wouldn't it be better if we just acted like those satsuma trees and produced fruit wherever we are planted?

Week 4:   Perform

Reflection: Don't wait for the perfect conditions … bear fruit now.

Scripture: Galatians 5:22–23

But the fruit of the Spirit is love, joy, peace, forbearance, kindness, goodness, faithfulness, gentleness and self-control. Against such things there is no law.

Pray/Meditate:

1. Spend a few minutes asking the Holy Spirit to reveal to you where your fruit is green and needs to ripen or mature.

2. Pray that spiritual fruit grows as a result of your Go Fish Project.

3. Pray that the global church would become known worldwide for demonstrating the fruits of the Spirit listed.

5:10 Task: Enjoy a piece of fruit at dinner, and decide what fruit of the Spirit each family member displays the most.

House Hunters

Raise your hand if you've heard this one before:

> Newlyweds David and Laura are moving from their cramped garage apartment at David's parents' house in Birmingham, Alabama. David's new job is taking the couple to Destin, Florida, and to the sun and surf he has always wanted—but will the pricey beachfront homes prove too much for Laura's frugal taste?

And just like that we are sucked into David and Laura's drama over buying a house. The marketing executives at HGTV are smart cookies. They have figured out that Americans prefer to purchase a home vicariously ... in about thirty minutes.

We soon find out the following:

> David desires an open floor plan to catch the breezes off the Gulf of Mexico, while Laura wants a spacious updated kitchen; David feels a roomy backyard for Marley, their yellow lab, would be best, but Laura is willing to sacrifice the yard for a garage.

And so the story unfolds. We know that at some point during the show, the responsible, practical one will express concern over costs, safety, or commute time, while the carefree partner typically says, "Yeah, but did you see that view!"

And that is the appeal of HGTV's *House Hunters*. The drama is a little fabricated, but we just want to be entertained. We really don't want to invest too much time or energy getting to know this couple—just enough to guess which house we think they are going to pick. We wonder if we could make the ideas we see on the show work in our own houses. We even get to travel to places we have never been. From the safe confines of our couches, we view other people living and doing and building … and then, we go to bed.

House Hunters is HGTV's version of a reality show, I get that. But are we filling our lives with this hollow entertainment? Are we developing quasi-relationships instead of fuller, richer ones? Are we using our leisure time watching others live instead of pursuing a deeper, more meaningful cause ourselves? Imagine how exciting life could be if Christians left the couch to renovate and build the lives of others.

Jesus promised us abundant life if we did. And he promised to help us too. But we have to make him the cornerstone of our lives. When he is the foundation, a house becomes a home—where families thrive and guests are welcome!

Week 4:	Perform
Reflection:	Stick around for the harvest.
Scripture:	Mark 4:13–20

Then Jesus said to them, "Don't you understand this parable? How then will you understand any parable? The farmer sows the word. Some people are like seed along the path, where the word is sown. As soon as they hear it, Satan comes and takes away the word that was sown in them. Others, like seed sown on rocky places, hear the word and at once receive it with joy. But since they have no root, they last only a short time. When trouble or persecution comes because of the word, they quickly fall away. Still others, like seed sown among thorns, hear the word; but the worries of this life, the deceitfulness of wealth and the desires for other things come in and choke the word, making it unfruitful. Others, like seed sown on good soil, hear the word, accept it, and produce a crop—some thirty, some sixty, some a hundred times what was sown."

Pray/Meditate:

1. Set a timer for five minutes. Devote those five minutes exclusively to the worship of our God. If your mind wanders, bring it back quickly to worship. Do not pray about yourself, your family, or even this project. You can quote Scripture, sing, hum—choose whatever methods allow you to worship. Hit the timer and go deep with God ...

2. Now that you are in the proper mind-set, promise God that you will spend the time to develop relationships with the people involved in this project. Ask him to produce soft, fertile soil that allows you to produce a harvest.

3. We must cultivate our hearts into fertile soil—capable of producing a crop worth a bountiful harvest. Pray for the harvest that will come from this project—that it might glorify God.

5:10 Task:	Fix something around the house that you have been meaning to fix!

I'm Not Dead Yet

In the summer of 1897, Samuel Langhorne Clemens, better known as Mark Twain, passed away ... or so it was reported. Because of Twain's immense popularity, rumors circulated quickly throughout the northeast.

None was more saddened and surprised to hear about this than Mark Twain himself.

So, in typical Mark Twain fashion, he jotted down a lengthy rebuttal to the *New York Journal* that was printed on June 2, 1897. The column explained that it was Twain's cousin, James Ross Clemens, who was actually ill, but you and I remember the last sentence: "The report of my death was greatly exaggerated."[29]

Believe it or not, premature obituaries are more common than you might think. On April 16, 2003, www.cnn.com posted memorials on notable figures Fidel Castro, Dick Cheney, Nelson Mandela, Bob Hope, Gerald Ford, Pope John Paul II, and Ronald Reagan—all of whom were living at the time. Whoops![30]

Notable rock band Kansas guitarist Rich Williams was reported as dust in the wind by several New England newspapers in 2009. It was actually Eric de Boer who died, a long-time *impersonator* of the famous guitarist.

Would you be surprised if the media ran an obituary on God? On his church? *Time Magazine* came close back on April 8, 1966, when their cover asked the question, "Is God Dead?" German philosopher Friedrich Nietzsche thought so. He wrote, "God is dead. God remains dead ... and

---

29   Shelley Fisher Fishkin, *Lighting Out For the Territory : Reflections on Mark Twain and American Culture* (Oxford University Press, 1996), p. 134
30   Sue Chan, *CNN Chagrined over Premature Obits*, http://www.cbsnews.com/news/cnn-chagrined-over-premature-obits/. April 17 2003.

what are these churches now if they are not the tombs and sepulchers of God?"[31]

So I ask you—was Nietzsche right? Is the church dead? Why would people think so? Could it be that we as Christians are not living proof?

Remember how to initiate cardiopulmonary resuscitation or CPR? The first step is to gently poke or prod the individual and ask him or her, "Are you okay?" If there is no response, resuscitation is necessary. Despite being shaken, poked, and prodded in the last fifty years, the church seems unresponsive. May I suggest that the church is in need of resuscitation? We need to shift our focus on demonstrating love into our communities rather than just being the squeaky wheel on Fox News.

Here's a little secret ... we are not dead yet. In fact, the church will never die. Jesus promised such when he told Peter that the gates of hell will not prevail against us. There is a day coming soon when we will all ride on horseback behind our leader, the Lord Jesus. He'll be easy to spot, mounted on his white horse, huge crown on his head, eyes blazing, his robe dipped in blood and emblazoned with his name: *King of Kings and Lord of Lords*. His mere words will slay the nations. On that day, no one will question the existence of he who is faithful and true or his church.

But why wait until then? Let us prove to the world that the reports of our death have been greatly exaggerated.

---

31   Fredrick Nietzsche, *Die fröhliche Wissenschaft. 1882.*

Week 4:	Perform
Reflection:	Never give up.
Scripture:	Revelation 19:11–16

I saw heaven standing open and there before me was a white horse, whose rider is called Faithful and True. With justice he judges and wages war. His eyes are like blazing fire, and on his head are many crowns. He has a name written on him that no one knows but he himself. He is dressed in a robe dipped in blood, and his name is the Word of God. The armies of heaven were following him, riding on white horses and dressed in fine linen, white and clean. Coming out of his mouth is a sharp sword with which to strike down the nations. "He will rule them with an iron scepter." He treads the winepress of the fury of the wrath of God Almighty. On his robe and on his thigh he has this name written: King of Kings and Lord of Lords.

Pray/Meditate:

1. Raise your hand if you've ever uttered these words: "I am so sick and tired of this world! I really just wish Jesus would come back today." That day is coming, but before it does, we have work to do. Pray for the Holy Spirit to reveal your part.

2. It is getting harder to live in our world as Christians ... but don't give up. Pray for courage and strength to live for God.

3. There is no better way to prove to the world that the church is still alive and well than to demonstrate Christ's love. Pray that your project will attract others to Christ to the glory of God.

5:10 Task: Go to www.youtube.com and type in "Final Minute—Miracle on Ice." Watch and remember ... never give up.

If at Hearse You Don't Succeed[32]

In the small towns of the rural South, public services are often stretched very thin in what they can provide. Providers of these services often have full-time regular jobs. For example, fire departments in most rural municipalities are volunteer. The hospital pathologist might also double as the county coroner and the town veterinarian the local taxidermist, that sort of thing. Service is provided but usually by a different route and at a different pace than typically experienced by those living in urban areas.

Such was the case one Saturday night in the tiny town of Hamilton, Georgia. Hamilton is so small that Third Street is on the edge of town.

When our friend Carolyn fell that night and hurt her back, she knew she needed emergency care beyond what Hamilton could provide. The discomfort was so wrenching, she had to lie flat, which meant an ambulance ride. She had her husband call the local ambulance service—thirty miles away—which, of course, knew them by name.

"Oh, Ray, tell Carolyn we can't get anybody out there to you," explained the local telephone operator and emergency dispatcher. "The ambulance is out right now and will be occupied for a while. I am so sorry."

"Well, what are we supposed to do? She's got to get to the emergency room," asked her husband.

"Hmmm ... you could try Jim over at the mortuary. He works with the ambulance folks a lot. Maybe they have an idea," offered the dispatcher.

Ray wasn't sure, but his wife was in so much pain that his options were limited. He called the mortuary service. It was obviously after hours, but

---

32 This experience is shared by Ray Smoot and dedicated to the memory of his wife, Carolyn. It is with great joy that I honor her by telling this story.

the owner was more than happy to help the family out. They dispatched a hearse right away.

"A *hearse*?" Carolyn questioned. But she was in so much pain, she conceded.

When the hearse arrived, Carolyn's husband noticed that the driver Jim sent had already started his Saturday-evening festivities before he got the call—he was three sheets to the wind. Ray shuddered when he thought of Carolyn riding in the hearse weaving down the county roads on the way to the hospital, so he convinced the driver to let him get behind the wheel.

So together, Ray and the driver strapped Carolyn down to the boards in the back of the hearse, and away they went. Along the way, Carolyn began to get hot and stuffy and asked Ray if he could turn on some air conditioning. But Ray, who was focused on driving the black behemoth, didn't want to take his hands off the ten o'clock and two o'clock positions. So Carolyn asked the driver, "Is there any way I can I can get some air back here?"

The inebriated driver confessed, "Lordy, Mrs. Carolyn, I don't rightly know. Ain't nobody from back there never asked that before!"

When Ray and the driver parked the hearse at the curb of the ER, they caused quite a stir in the waiting room. Was this a pick up or drop off? Either way, the crowd was unsettled.

When the unlikely duo carried Carolyn in through the double doors, they were quickly greeted by the triage nurse. "Sir, the morgue is around back."

Carolyn propped herself up on her elbows and said, "No. I'm glad to be here. That ride was killing me!"

As crazy as the journey was to get there, Ray had gotten the job done.

Week 4:   Perform

Reflection: Whatever it takes, get the job done.

Scripture: Mark 2:2–5, 11

> They gathered in such large numbers that there was no room left, not even outside the door, and he preached the word to them. Some men came, bringing to him a paralyzed man, carried by four of them. Since they could not get him to Jesus because of the crowd, they made an opening in the roof above Jesus by digging through it and then lowered the mat the man was lying on. When Jesus saw their faith, he said to the paralyzed man, "Son, your sins are forgiven … I tell you, get up, take your mat and go home."

Pray/Meditate:

1. Today's story about the "ambulance" ride reminds us that sometimes in order to get things done, we have to be creative. Sometimes that means changing your plan. As you go deeper into your Go Fish Project, pray for wisdom in case you have to tweak the plan.

2. The paralytic's friends in today's Scripture went to every door and every window to gain an audience with Jesus. The friends couldn't go around, through, or under the crowds, so they went over them … on the roof. Pray for persistence today when the project becomes a little difficult.

3. Finally, let's put aside the project and talk about you just a minute. Are you in need of a creative approach to God? Do you need persistence in your spiritual life? Pray for the Spirit to indwell you with a fresh perspective and renewed energy to serve our Lord.

5:10 Task: Recall a time when you came up with a creative solution to a problem. If you are more persistent than creative, remember a time when your persistence paid off. Whatever your response, share with a friend and ask him or her the same question.

WEEK 5

Week 5—Perform

What Would You Do?

A friend of mine, Owen Bailey, is a healthcare executive who understands employee culture. He knows from experience that leaders who provide the right environment for employees to excel in their jobs reap the benefits of an engaged workforce.

Every so often he has all his employees answer the following question, "If I were CEO, I would …" The answers range from the obscure to the obvious, but more than anything, the exercise lets employees know that he is listening. A connection is developed that opens the door for better communication and a deeper understanding between senior leaders and staff.

Today I would like to ask you a similar question. "If you were in charge of the church, what would you do?" If we were honest with each other, I am sure we could all come up with a laundry list of things to improve the church. Really, though, are we the right people to ask? What if we asked our communities what they needed and if anything, what they thought the church could provide?

It turns out, someone already has, and the answers might surprise you.

In 2011, the Barna Group asked that very question to over one thousand people in various communities. To get a better feel for the two perspectives involved, the Barna Group divided the pollsters into two categories—the churched and the unchurched.

The church folk responded that they could help the community with poverty (31 percent) and that the communities could benefit from churches providing places to worship (18 percent) and from spiritual growth and Bible study (18 percent). The unchurched in the community disagreed.

The majority of the respondents in this category, over 33 percent, felt that the church offered *nothing* that could help the community.[33]

Ouch. Talk about a wake-up call. Is there any wonder why the church is seen as out of touch and socially irrelevant? If this attitude prevails, we will isolate ourselves into obscurity. What is the answer, then? It is relatively simple. We just need to imitate our Father. He took the initiative to provide salvation once and for all people. As His children, we should extend the same mercy and hope into our communities and let the Lord take care of the rest. He will sort out the results in His own time. Our calling is to go.

When my friend Owen asks the question of his employees, he takes some hits from the skeptics. But it doesn't deter him because he knows that in the long run, he is modeling good leadership. As we go out into the community, we should do the same—model our leader.

---

33   Source: Barna Group. OmniPoll; Do Churches Contribute to Communities? *What does your community need, if anything, that you feel churches could provide?* www. barna.org. February 2011.

Week 5:	Perform
Reflection:	Go do something.
Scripture:	Romans 5:8; Ephesians 5:1–2

But God demonstrates his own love for us in this: While we were still sinners, Christ died for us. (Romans 5:8)

Therefore be imitators of God, as beloved children; and walk in love, just as Christ also loved you and gave himself up for us, an offering and a sacrifice to God as a fragrant aroma. (Ephesians 5:1–2)

Pray/Meditate:

1. Reflect for a moment on why you think that 33 percent of the unchurched in the Barna Group poll think that there is nothing the church can do in their community. Pray for forgiveness for the church in that regard.

2. As your group performs your Go Fish Project, listen for cues on what the community is saying about the church. Pray for the unity of the church to address them.

3. Read John 15:5 and ask the Spirit, "What would I do if *you* were in charge?"

5:10 Task: Search www.youtube.com for "Matthew West *Do Something* official video." Watch and enjoy.

Why Men Grill

The first six months with our second son, Sam, were a lot different than with our first son, Britton. My wife and I welcomed Sam into the world thinking that with twenty-one months of practice already under our belt with his brother, this was going to be a piece of cake.

But there was the NICU the first night he was born. Then came the jaundice. Then the finishing blow—colic. Remember that story in Luke 9 where Jesus came down from the mountain and the man greeted him by saying, "Teacher, I beg you to look at my son ... a spirit seizes him and he suddenly screams; it throws him into convulsions so that he foams at the mouth ... I begged your disciples to drive it out, but they could not."

I feel pretty sure the kid in Luke had colic.

Sam's colic lasted for months. That's right, months. At least I could go to work. My wife was exhausted from dealing with it on a daily basis. Which is why when I came home one day from work in the middle of Sam's afternoon fit, she begged me to hold him while she could at least enjoy a peaceful and relaxing shower for a few minutes. I was more than happy to oblige.

Sam and I had figured out that if I laid him on his belly along the length of my forearm, this would help. He spent much of those colicky months looking at the ground, dangling like a cheetah asleep in a tree.

But that evening, he was wound up. No position, no music, no rocking could alleviate his pain or the ear-piercing screams echoing in our house. I wanted my wife to enjoy her brief solace, so I closed all the doors to trap the sound.

Desperate, I looked for something to take Sam's mind off the pain in his tummy. Aha! The old chandelier with the fake candles in our living room! It was shiny and bright and just might do the trick.

I quickly walked over to the light and held Sam up so he could see it better. Instead, as I raised him to the light, it startled him. He drew his arms in, but not before his right wrist made contact with a very hot bulb on one of the candles. Reflexively, he swung his arm to avoid the pain, causing the chandelier to spin ... which caused another very hot bulb to contact his right cheek.

I drew Sam back in horror. The screams approached dangerous decibels. And there, with her hair dripping wet, stood Christy in her bathrobe watching the whole thing.

"What have you done to my child?" she asked.

"I ... I was just trying to ... I didn't mean ..." was all I could muster.

"What happened? He has a blister on his cheek!" She pointed to his wrist. "And his wrist too? What did you do? Never mind, I'll take care of him."

She took him from me with a look of contempt. "All I wanted was ten minutes of peace. Get the hamburger meat off the counter in the kitchen and go grill. Try not to burn yourself."

Ouch.

After a few hours, Christy and I mended fences. I held Sam again later that night but avoided quick movements and bright lights. Mistakes happen. Don't let them cause you to pull back from what you are supposed to be doing.

Week 5:	Perform
Reflection:	Mistakes may happen … keep serving anyway.
Scripture:	Luke 22:54–62

Then seizing him, they led him away and took him into the house of the high priest. Peter followed at a distance. And when some there had kindled a fire in the middle of the courtyard and had sat down together, Peter sat down with them. A servant girl saw him seated there in the firelight. She looked closely at him and said, "This man was with him." But he denied it. "Woman, I don't know him," he said. A little later someone else saw him and said, "You also are one of them." "Man, I am not!" Peter replied. About an hour later another asserted, "Certainly this fellow was with him, for he is a Galilean." Peter replied, "Man, I don't know what you're talking about!" Just as he was speaking, the rooster crowed. The Lord turned and looked straight at Peter. Then Peter remembered the word the Lord had spoken to him: "Before the rooster crows today, you will disown me three times." And he went outside and wept bitterly.

Pray/Meditate:

1. Spend a moment reflecting on what Peter must have felt when realized what he had done. Then read Acts 2:14. Peter got back in the game. Is there something in your past that you need to let go of to get back in the game? Pray for insight to do so.

2. Read Genesis 50:19–21. Ask for the Spirit to give you a faith like Joseph. He was obedient to God in all kinds of difficulty, and by the end of his life, he saw God's hand throughout his life.

3. Making mistakes means you are actively living out your faith. Pray that God will use your human effort—the good and the bad—for his glory during this project.

| **5:10 Task:** | Read the quote from President Teddy Roosevelt found at: www.theodore-roosevelt.com/trsorbonnespeech.html. |

<u>This Is Humiliating</u>

"I'm breaking up with you, and if you think we are getting back together, then you've got a long road ahead of you." I actually said those words to a former girlfriend. I was a real Casanova.

There are a few possibilities for why I would say such a hurtful thing. Perhaps I was trying to compensate for my macho-lacking name (more on this in devotion 36). Maybe I was feeling the pressure of trying to get into graduate school. Could be that I was scared of defining the relationship further. Whatever the reason I rationalized in my head that day, it wasn't justified.

Funny thing is that the girl was awesome. To this day, I have never enjoyed the whole dating thing more than with her. We had so much fun together. She was everything I was not. I was focused, disciplined, and determined. She filled in my gaps and my blind spots. If you are a fan of Harry Potter, she was my Luna Lovegood.

So what drove me to break up with this girl? I wrestled with my decision the weeks following the break up, and I kept coming back to our differences. As I said, she was Luna. Carefree, without a plan, spontaneous, and quirky. If I stayed with her, I feared my life would spiral out of control.

I learned a lot through that breakup. What I discovered about myself was something that God had been trying to teach me for years. He was in control, not me. Control is such an illusion. I figured out that having everything figured out leaves little room for faith. We all want to end up in the driver's seat of our lives, achieving mapped-out checkpoints to know when we have arrived. All the while, Jesus patiently sits in the passenger seat, hoping that we will exit onto the straight and narrow path with Him. But we've got to reach our destination ...

Truth is, our destination should be to take a journey with the Lord.

Paul just thought he was living until Jesus flashed His lights at him on the Damascus road. Humiliated, he had to be led by hand as he groveled into Damascus. When you are truly humble, though, the Lord takes your hand and leads you to places you would ordinarily never go. Life's journey becomes deeper, richer, and fuller. Once he let Jesus drive, Paul was happy to live in that humility and that weakness. I can identify with Paul—both of us have control issues.

I hurt a girl very deeply because of my desire to be in control. So I groveled back to her, humiliated. Twenty-five years later, I'm glad I did. Love you, Luna.

Week 5:   Perform

Reflection: Humility works just fine in God's Kingdom

Scripture: 2 Corinthians 12:9–10

But he said to me, "My grace is sufficient for you, for my power is made perfect in weakness." Therefore I will boast all the more gladly about my weaknesses, so that Christ's power may rest on me. That is why, for Christ's sake, I delight in weaknesses, in insults, in hardships, in persecutions, in difficulties. For when I am weak, then I am strong.

Pray/Meditate:

1. Read Colossians 1:15–17 and then Philippians 2:8. Reflect on the humility it took for Christ to allow Himself to be nailed to be crucified.

2. Humility in the Christian sense has less to do with meekness and gentleness and more to do with handing over our will to God. Pray that the Holy Spirit will point out where humility is necessary in your life to find God's will for you.

3. Pray for humility as you finish the Go Fish Project so you deflect any glory received to our Father.

5:10 Task: Be humble in your dealings with people today—regardless of who's right and who's wrong.

The Cone of Probability

People who live along the Southern Gulf Coast are very familiar with hurricanes.

We keep one eye on the weather and one eye on our normal lives when these storms are in the Gulf of Mexico, but in order for hurricanes to gain our full attention, two questions must be answered:

1. Are we in the cone of probability?

2. Has anyone spotted Jim Cantore from the Weather Channel?

If we get an affirmative answer on both questions, then we know it's time to batten down the hatches.

For hurricanes, the cone of probability accurately predicts whether the storm is headed your direction within a certain time frame. This is extremely important to look for during hurricane season.

Christians will soon find themselves smack in the middle of a different cone of probability in the coming years. That cone is predicting an increase in religious activity in America. And Christians will play a vital role in deciding what type of activity that will be.

There are three main reasons why this will happen. First, the youngest baby boomers just celebrated their fiftieth birthday during 2014. Nearly ten thousand members of this generation will turn sixty-five every day for the next fifteen years. That is important because each generation prior to the Boomers has become more religious as they get older. If this generation continues in that trend, a large, positive religious movement could happen.

Second, the population of the United States continues to migrate toward states that are more religious. As the ratio of people exposed to a Christian culture increases, churches that are prepared for this influx can sow a bountiful harvest.

And finally, those under thirty-five years old are seeking more of a nontraditional religious experience. They want their churches to be more socially relevant. They are challenging their churches to find ways to extend their beliefs into their communities and thus provide tangible evidence of their faith. I believe going out into the community provides the perfect intersection to revive traditional churches and meet the needs of this younger generation.

These three trends should be really exciting to Christians. The church in America can deepen our nation's spiritual roots if we are found faithful. If we are not, then religious offshoots like new age movements, eastern religions, or other mysticisms will take our place. Christians know that there is no substitute for having a relationship with our Creator.

The forecast calls for heightened spiritual awareness in the coming years. Pray that committed Christians lead those seeking shelter from the storm into the gracious comfort of our Savior.

Week 5:   Perform

Reflection: Go into the community so others can come into your fellowship.

Scripture: Luke 17:7–10

"Suppose one of you has a servant plowing or looking after the sheep. Will he say to the servant when he comes in from the field, 'Come along now and sit down to eat'? Won't he rather say, 'Prepare my supper, get yourself ready and wait on me while I eat and drink; after that you may eat and drink'? Will he thank the servant because he did what he was told to do? So you also, when you have done everything you were told to do, should say, 'We are unworthy servants; we have only done our duty.'"

Pray/Meditate:

1. The first time I read today's verses, I thought they were kind of harsh toward the servant. As I got older, I realized that Jesus was simply giving a concrete example of how we should approach our acts of service. Christians are called to be servant leaders, servant spouses, servant family members, servant employees—you get the idea. Service should be part of our DNA. Pray that your acts of service are acceptable to our Lord.

2. The best way to become proficient at service is to practice it. That is the reasoning behind the Go Fish Project—practice what you preach! Pray that Christians will accept the challenge of the coming spiritual wave with a servant's heart.

3. Pray to the Holy Spirit for insight on how to match your individual gifts with acts of service.

5:10 Task: Perform an act of service for someone who needs your help today.

I Want to Be Like Them ...

When Christy and I brought Britton, our firstborn, home from the hospital, I just had one rule for dressing him: no frilly one-piece stuff with collars or lace at any time. Thinking we would have a daughter in the mix at some point, Christy relented but with a caveat. She could pull out the occasional pleated, fancy attire up until the age of two. We shook on it and moved on.

Then came Samuel. Then Jack. Christy's visions of princesses and glass slippers at the ball were fading fast. When she realized Jack was going to be the caboose of the children, I would love to tell you that she loaded up on the smocked clothing, but like a trooper, she kept her end of the bargain ... except for the Easter of 2001 incident.

In the spring of 2001, Britton and Sam breathed a sigh of relief. At six and four, respectively, they were out of range. Technically thirty months, but still a solid two in Christy's mind, poor Jack, however, found himself square in the middle of his mother's fashion crosshairs. It was his last Easter at age two, and Christy planned on taking full advantage of it.

Easter morning we dressed for church. Britton and I high-fived over his neatly pressed khaki shorts, cream-colored polo-style shirt, dapper little white socks, and bucks. Sam donned the same outfit, only one size smaller.

And then, there was Jack. Christy gushed over his cuteness, but I could tell Jack felt like Ralphie in *A Christmas Story* wearing the pink bunny suit from Aunt Clara. The other boys snickered. I quickly left the room to brush my teeth. Jack cried and pitched a fit. Christy said, "Jack, you wear that or nothing at all!" He stormed out of the room.

He reemerged a few minutes later wearing only a diaper, white socks, and Sunday shoes. "And just where is your outfit, Jack?" his mother asked.

"Me no like!" Jack emphatically pronounced. In only two years, he had already figured out that he wanted to follow the example of his older and much better-dressed brothers.

The Go Fish Project is designed to be an example of how to demonstrate Christ's love into the community. It is a simple model that can be repeated over and over with various groups. The goal is to repeat the pattern enough so that both church members and the nonchurched can see concrete examples of what Christianity truly looks like.

Jesus came to earth to fish and to teach us how to fish as well. Why else would he ask his disciples to follow him and become fishers of men? Jesus started a movement by setting an example to his disciples. He was constantly fishing for the lost, the poor, the weak, and the weary. Through the ages and with God's help, Christians have drawn others into the faith by following the example of Jesus. The more each of us follows His example, the more vibrant the church becomes. When the church becomes stale, ineffective, or isolated, it is because we are following an example other than Christ.

When Jack was two, he looked around to see who he wanted to be like. I am thankful that Jack has two older Christian brothers who are a good example for him. What about you? Are you a good example? Are you modeling the behaviors of Christ?

Week 5:	Perform
Reflection:	Reflect the Lord so that others want to be like you.
Scripture:	1 Corinthians 11:1; Philippians 3:16–17

Follow my example, as I follow the example of Christ. (1 Corinthians 11:1)

Only let us live up to what we have already attained. [17] Join together in following my example, brothers and sisters, and just as you have us as a model, keep your eyes on those who live as we do. (Philippians 3:16–17)

Pray/Meditate:

1. Reflect for a moment on whether or not Christendom would be strengthened or weakened if believers followed your example. Pray for the Holy Spirit to guide you to truth as you reflect.

2. Read Galatians 5:22–23—which of these fruits are exemplary in your life? Great! Which need prayer? Pray for them!

3. Pray that you and your group will demonstrate the love of Christ in such a way that others are drawn to Jesus during this project.

5:10 Task: Call, text, or e-mail someone who has been a good example for you! Thank them!

The Tables at Waffle House

Wouldn't it be great if the tables at Waffle House were bigger?

I know that is a really deep thought to start off today's devotional, but think about it. How many of you have jostled drinks, silverware, and plates to get everything situated just right, only to have the waitress bring the last plate of toast to put on the table?

A bigger table would be nice.

For years we have heard pastors and theologians tell us the same thing about God. Maybe not the table reference but that our concept of God needs to be bigger. They urge us not to put God in a box. To think such a thing is to deny the awesome capability of our Lord. He is too vast and too powerful to be confined to such small spaces. Guess he wouldn't fit around a Waffle House table, huh?

We all agree that God is beyond the limited scope of our thinking. He is able to do more than we can possibly imagine. Perhaps we have reduced him to a pocket deity that we take out each Sunday and pay him just enough tribute to ease our guilt over our shallow faith. A.W. Tozer saw this coming when he described Christians in *The Pursuit of God*:

> We now demand glamour and fast-flowing dramatic action. A generation of Christians reared among push buttons and automatic machines is impatient of slower and less direct methods of reaching their goals ... The tragic results of this spirit all about us: shallow lives, hollow religious philosophies ... the glorification of men, trust is religious externalities ... salesmanship methods, the mistaking of dynamic personality for the power of

the Spirit. These and such of these are the symptoms of an evil disease.[34]

What makes this quote even more remarkable is that Tozer wrote it nearly seventy years ago!

God isn't limited by the size of the box in which we carry him. He is limited because we've elbowed him out of our lives. He doesn't want to be bigger; he wants to be cherished. Before he can do great things with us, he wants to know that he can trust us in the small. We share big news with just about anybody, but the most intimate details of our lives are reserved for our closest friends. Shouldn't God be the one we share with the most?

Come to think of it, I think the snug fit of Waffle House tables is just perfect for God. That way, we share everything and get to know each other up close and personal—just the way he likes it.

---

34 A. W. Tozer, *The Pursuit of God*. (Harrisburg, PA: Christian Publications, Inc., 1948), 67.

Week 5: Perform

Reflection: God may be big, but he wants to be with us in the small.

Scripture: 1 Kings 19:11–13

The Lord said, "Go out and stand on the mountain in the presence of the Lord, for the Lord is about to pass by." Then a great and powerful wind tore the mountains apart and shattered the rocks before the Lord, but the Lord was not in the wind. After the wind there was an earthquake, but the Lord was not in the earthquake. After the earthquake came a fire, but the Lord was not in the fire. And after the fire came a gentle whisper. When Elijah heard it, he pulled his cloak over his face and went out and stood at the mouth of the cave.

Pray/Meditate:

1. There is no better way to have an intimate relationship with our Lord than to spend quality time with him in prayer. Not the falling asleep laundry list prayer or the I'm in a pickle plea but regular, devoted time to listen to him without interruptions. So for today, practice quiet conversation with God.

2. Actually talk, even whisper your prayer today. Saying a prayer out loud keeps our minds on track a little better. Ask questions of God as you speak to him. It is a conversation, not a monologue.

3. Pray for God's intimate touch on your Go Fish Project. Pray that he is so near that people see him through you and your team.

5:10 Task: Call, text, or e-mail your best friends today. Thank them for being so close.

A Sense of Community

There is something really special about living in a small town. Sure, we may sacrifice some conveniences like shopping and restaurants, but the trade-offs make it worthwhile.

My wife Christy and I we were reminded of what it is like to be a part of a small community the other day on our 6:15 a.m. morning walk. It went something like this …

Just down from our house, we usually run into Joey and Kim, who are out walking their foster dogs. Leaving them, we regularly overtake ninety-one-year-old Ms. Daphne, who is returning from her morning walk to McDonald's for coffee. She warns us of a pile of bamboo that the city failed to pick up yesterday on up ahead.

On this particular morning, our good friend Owen Bailey honks at us as he passes. It is too early for him to be going to work, and he is in his wife Genie's car. "Wonder what he's doing," I ask Christy.

She doesn't answer me because she's focused on a fast-approaching runner. It's Dr. Amy Christmas—the local ophthalmologist. My wife calls out, "Morning! I didn't recognize you for a second!"

"I can help with that," she says as she speeds by.

We all chuckle. At the next crosswalk, I notice Paul, a city public works employee, waiting for a red light to change. "Hey, there is a pile of bamboo back on Fairhope Av—"

Before I can finish, he interrupts. "Ms. Daphne's already called."

My wife uses the opportunity to ask Paul about the city's summer flower arrangements. "What happened to the zinnias this year?"

The light changes, so Paul can't answer, but he promises to tell us tomorrow. Passing the post office, we see Owen returning to his house. He slows down enough to show us a bag of McGriddles and says, "Charlie's birthday."

We finally make it into town. "Asleep or awake?" I ask my wife.

"I say awake," my wife answers. She knows I am referring to Matisse, the cat that lounges in a store-front window downtown. We peek in the window.

"Is she awake?" asks a familiar voice from across the street. It is Lisa Brodie, who has just returned from her mission trip to Tanzania.

"Asleep ... like you should be. Aren't you still on Africa time?" my wife answers.

And so it goes, as our thirty-minute walk turns into forty-five. That is the trade-off of living in a small community, but I wouldn't have it any other way.

Statistics reveal that only one in five American churches is flourishing.[35] That is really sad, but honestly, not surprising. Growing churches have similar traits that distinguish them from the 80 percent that are not, no matter where they are located or what size they are. One of those traits is the way they approach relationships.

Growing churches go out of their way to build community within their ranks and just as importantly, beyond their walls. They take the Great Commission literally and build lasting relationships as they go. This is exactly the pattern revealed to us in the book of Acts as the early church scattered from Jerusalem.

The Go Fish Project is designed to demonstrate the love of Christ and along the way build relationships between churches and their communities. Both are strengthened in the process. Although we are nearing the official end to your Go Fish Project, I hope the sense of community developed over these forty days makes a lasting impact on you, your partner, and your team.

It certainly did for the original twelve who answered Jesus' call to go fish ...

35   Rebecca Barnes and Lindy Lowry, *7 Startling Facts: An up close look at church attendance in America.* http://www.churchleaders.com/pastors/pastor-articles/139575-7-startling-facts-an-up-close-look-at-church-attendance-in-america.html

Week 5:	Perform
Reflection:	Demonstrating Christ's love builds community.
Scripture:	Revelation 21:3–4

And I heard a loud voice from the throne saying, "Look! God's dwelling place is now among the people, and he will dwell with them. They will be his people, and God himself will be with them and be their God. He will wipe every tear from their eyes. There will be no more death or mourning or crying or pain, for the old order of things has passed away."

Pray/Meditate:

1. Today's verses speak of a future date for us to look forward to as Christians. The new community described will be inhabited by our Lord himself. Reflect for a moment on how awesome that will be.

2. Pray that community was developed during your Go Fish Project and that Christ's love was demonstrated in a mighty way.

3. Pray for your community and your church for continued opportunities to build each other up.

5:10 Task: Call, text, or e-mail a neighbor that you haven't spoken to in a while. Reestablish a sense of community with him or her.

WEEK 6

Week 6—Praise!

Team Meeting 5

Step 1   Take five minutes and ask everyone to reflect on his or her opinion of the project. Discuss any insights your team members gained during this final week through the devotionals, the project work, or the relationships encountered.

Step 2   Pray a thanksgiving prayer for the work completed and relationships made!

Step 3   Upload team photos if you haven't done so already.

Step 4   As your project winds down, also include pictures of the project and upload at www.gofishproject.com. (Be sure it is okay with participants to use photos on the web.) When you upload your photos, you can also provide a brief description of your project on the webpage as well under the "Team Information" tab.

Step 5   Celebrate together!

Looking forward ... did this GFP open doors to build bridges into your community? Then do it again!

What's in a Name?

In the Bible, names matter. God changed Abram's name to Abraham, which means *father of many*; Jesus changed Simon's name to Peter or Petra, which means *rock*; and of course, Jesus or Yeshua means *the Lord is salvation*. In Antioch, the largest church in the New Testament, followers of Jesus were first given the name Christians.

Although she was a very devout woman, my mother did not refer to the Scriptures to name her children. Instead she used alliteration—each of our names starts with the same letter.

So as the youngest, when my mom was deciding on a name for me, she had one rule—it had to begin with the letter K. My older brother, Kirk, started the trend—a strong, bold name for the firstborn male. A nice choice by my mom. Second came my sister, Kelly, a name that was steadily gaining popularity throughout the 1960s. A little cutting edge, Mom, very good.

Then it was my turn.

If you read the cover of this book, you realize my given name is Kerry. I wish, oh how I wish, that this was just my pen name. Unfortunately, it is real. I asked my mother once why she saddled me with such a name. Here was her line of thinking, and I quote, "Well, I think it is a pretty name. We didn't have ultrasound back in those days, so I thought Kerry would be a good name in case you were a boy or a girl."

Dear woman, may I point out the flaw in your logic? Wouldn't it have been better to have two names picked out, say Kevin and Katie? Talk about your square peg round hole! Hence, I was assigned to the transgender name club forever.

Now, before you rush to the side of my mother and defend her choice, let me point out one other factor. Our last name is Flowers. Kerry Flowers. A boy. No … just no. And where was my dad in all this? When the doctor came out to the waiting room and said, "Mr. Flowers, congratulations! You have a healthy baby boy named Kerry!" his response should have been, "No, his name is Kodiak." All the men in the room would have given my dad a cigar for that one!

Have you heard the song "A Boy Named Sue" by Johnny Cash? I lived it.

My wife and I met in college working at the university's recreation center, and she later confessed that when she signed up to work a shift with "Kerry Flowers," she thought it was a girl. Luckily, we went on to have a happy marriage, including three strapping sons named Dana, Pat, and Ashley. (Kidding.)

All this to say, having the name Kerry Flowers has provided many memorable situations over the years. Once someone meets me, though, they usually remember me as the guy with the girl's name. I am easily identified and remembered the next time.

Christians in Antioch were easily identified and remembered by their new name. Christians, or literally *Christ's people*, established Antioch as the hub of what Luke calls *the way*—supplanting Jerusalem as the center for church activity. Missionaries used Antioch as a springboard into Europe.

To go along with that new name, Christ's people had a passion for God, a passion for people, and a passion for a cause—to make Him known.

Today we still carry the name Christian … but I wonder, do we still have the same passion?

Week 6:	Praise!
Reflection:	Thank God for your identity in Him.
Scripture:	Acts 11:25–26; 1 Peter 4:16

Then Barnabas went to Tarsus to look for Saul, and when he found him, he brought him to Antioch. So for a whole year Barnabas and Saul met with the church and taught great numbers of people. The disciples were called Christians first at Antioch. (Acts 11:25–26)

However, if you suffer as a Christian, do not be ashamed, but praise God that you bear that name. (1 Peter 4:16)

Pray/Meditate:

1. Today's verses represent the only two times that the word *Christian* is used in the New Testament. Pray we will act like those first-century Christians and live up to our name.

2. Philippians 2:10 says, "That at the *name* of Jesus every knee shall bow in heaven and on earth and under the earth, and every tongue confess that Jesus Christ is Lord to the glory of God the Father." Pray to him whose name is above all names today. Thank him for his sacrifice, which earned you a birthright into his family.

3. As you wrap up your Go Fish Project this week, thank God for the opportunity to demonstrate the love of Christ in your community.

5:10 Task:	Go to YouTube and type in "Casting Crowns—Who Am I? Official Music Video." Watch and enjoy!

Week 6—Praise

There's No Crying in Baseball

In the movie *A League of their Own*, Tom Hanks plays baseball manager Jimmy Dugan, hired to coach an all-women's baseball team during World War II. Used to dealing with men all the time, he is not prepared for the emotional aspect that the women bring to the game. During one point during the film, Dugan criticizes Evelyn, a player who has just made a mental error. When she responds by crying, Dugan becomes exasperated and says, "Are you crying? Are you crying? There's no crying in baseball!"

Obviously Jimmy Dugan never coached seven- and eight-year-old boys. Being the father of three boys, I am all too familiar with it.

When my son Britton was eight, he was part of a pretty good team. Family friend Ralph Watson, who coached basketball in high school, was the head coach of the team. Ralph saw to it that the boys were technically sound, in the right position at all times, and prepared for any situations that might arise. My role was twofold: since it was coach-pitch league, I had to pitch to the boys when we were hitting, and I had to maintain the delicate emotional balance of seven- and eight-year-olds. I definitely drew the short end of the stick.

We started the season slow, but by the time playoffs rolled around, we were clicking on all cylinders. Individual team members knew their respective roles, and we really gelled as a group. We capped off a great season by making it to the league championship game.

The championship game started beautifully. We jumped out to an early lead, and the team was all cheers and smiles. But about the fifth inning, the wheels came off. The other team scored a couple of runs and was threatening with more. Our team was looking to the dugout for direction. I suggested rock, paper, scissors to determine if Ralph or I would have to be Dr. Phil. To keep their frail psyche intact, Ralph thought it would be smarter if the assistant coach trotted out there to give the boys the impression that this was no big deal. Chicken.

When I arrived at the pitcher's mound, the situation was critical. The whole infield was crying.

They say there is a fine line between crying and laughing, so I tried to flip them toward laughter. "Boys, your play right now is a little shaky. But it will in no way impact your standing at the concession stand. Each of you is still eligible for a small snack and a drink after the game, but unless we get an out here, I can't promise the drink offer is still on the table."

My son Britton was familiar with my shenanigans—he wasn't fooled. "Dad," he said, sobbing, "we need an out."

I looked at each one of them. Tears spilled out of their eyes and left clean streaks down their clay-covered cheeks. They were pitiful and in desperate need of assurance.

I knelt down and shifted tactics. I made them take their hands out of their gloves and put them together in the center of our circle. I told them what fun I had coaching them this year and how awesome it was going to be for the team to hold the championship trophy later that afternoon. I reminded them that we only needed two more outs to make it happen. And I trotted off.

Two outs later, we hoisted the trophy.

Week 6:	Praise!
Reflection:	When Christian teams play together, the joy experienced is as close to heaven as we get here on earth!
Scripture:	Philippians 1:3–6

I thank my God every time I remember you. In all my prayers for all of you, I always pray with joy because of your partnership in the gospel from the first day until now, being confident of this, that he who began a good work in you will carry it on to completion until the day of Christ Jesus.

Pray/Meditate:

1. The baseball team in today's story experienced ups and downs, but it was the downs that got them into trouble. When things seemed to be spinning out of control, the emotions spilled over, clouding their view of a special moment. Pull back from the Go Fish Project and see the bigger picture. God is the manager of the winning team. Thank him for adding you to the team; pray for trust as he manages you.

2. Paul's letter to the Philippians is unlike his communications with other churches. It reads more like a thank-you note. The reason is that the church at Philippi was acting like a church should. They had generously supported those in need, including Paul, and they were united as a team in their service to the Lord. Thank God for your Go Fish Project team. Pray also for a united church to act like a team and demonstrate the love of Christ.

3. Pray for other Go Fish Project teammates in different cities, states, and nations that are also doing projects—may the world see God through our team efforts.

| **5:10 Task:** | Thank your Go Fish Partner for his/her involvement in the project and for being on your team. |

Crustaceans at Christmas

The older I get, the more I like Christmas. I know, I know that sounds backward because nobody loves Christmas more than kids, right? But I think as I age, I appreciate the finite gift of time. The family nucleus of five that I grew up in has now expanded to nearly twenty, and soon we will have to abandon meeting at my parents' house when grandkids have their own kids and family responsibilities.

But as the youngest child of my parents, I get energized from the social aspect of Christmas. I selfishly don't want it to end. It's too much fun. And each year, traditions play a huge part in creating special memories.

My brother Kirk, the oldest sibling, decided it would be a great idea to give the family a present each year—a jigsaw puzzle—which we put together during our visit. So that has become a tradition. One night we'll squish into my parents' den like a pile of puppies to watch whatever movie came out on DVD for Christmas that year. And because we live in the Deep South, the weather usually allows us to walk around the outdoor mall in my hometown to spend our newly minted gift cards.

Far and away my favorite tradition, though, is the Christmas crustacean supper. The supper dates back to when my dad worked at a CPA firm. As an accountant in a small town, payment for services rendered sometimes included the barter system.

One client, a local seafood distributor, paid my dad's firm in fresh shrimp.

I'm not sure when exactly my mom decided to start the ritual, but for those of us along the Gulf Coast, nothing is better than fried shrimp, potato salad, baked beans, and if my mom is feeling spunky, cheese grits.

Feeding nearly twenty people that much food requires time and planning, so it's usually a day or two after Christmas before my mom can regroup a little. As much as we can fit into the cramped kitchen, we all help at various stages of the preparation. (For those in my family reading this, please play along that the men in the family actually help. I'm trying to create the illusion of a warm family atmosphere here.)

One man who actually does his job every year is my eighty-one-year-old dad. He usually de-heads and washes the shrimp in the morning and cranks up the deep fryer in the afternoon. By 6:00 p.m., after standing at the stove for hours frying dozens of the succulent seafood and fending off those of us who buzz by attempting to sample, his feeble little legs are shaking.

But once the preparations are complete, he still musters up enough strength to pray for the meal as we all gather in the kitchen.

The table is set. The smells float around the house. Family laughter fills the room. It is a tradition I don't want to see end. I wish you could come, too. And maybe you can … for one day, after this life is over, we'll all be reunited at the marriage supper of the Lamb. Who else needs to come?

Week 6:   Praise!

Reflection: All deserve to come to the wedding supper of the Lamb. Have you hand delivered your invitations?

Scripture: Revelation 19:5–9

> Then a voice came from the throne, saying: "Praise our God, all you his servants, you who fear him, both great and small! Then I heard what sounded like a great multitude, like the roar of rushing waters and like loud peals of thunder, shouting: "Hallelujah! For our Lord God Almighty reigns. Let us rejoice and be glad and give him glory. For the wedding of the Lamb has come, and his bride has made herself ready. Fine linen, bright and clean, was given her to wear." (Fine linen stands for the righteous acts of God's holy people.) Then the angel said to me, "Write this: Blessed are those who are invited to the wedding supper of the Lamb!" And he added, "These are the true words of God."

Pray/Meditate:

1. Pray that the efforts during your Go Fish Project will cause someone to RSVP to the supper of the Lamb! Pray that seeds planted during these forty days will bring about a harvest to the glory of God.

2. Spend a minute thinking about the moment when Jesus personally hands you your bright and clean linen to wear at his supper. Pray for the Spirit to reveal to you what you can do to hear Jesus say, "Well done, good and faithful servant!"

3. What traditions can your church start that will invite more people to the marriage supper of the Lamb? Reflect on this, and write an idea down to share with church leaders.

5:10 Task: Get the family together and discuss your favorite Christmas family traditions. If you don't have any, come up with one to start this year.

<u>Jubilee!</u>

During the summer of 2001, a job change required our family to move to Fairhope, Alabama—a small town on the eastern shore of Mobile Bay. Upon moving there, we heard of a rare, unusual phenomenon that occurs during the summer in Mobile Bay but only along the eastern shore. It is called a jubilee.

Without getting all scientific, a jubilee is when sea life that normally dwell on the bottom of the bay follow oxygen pockets to the surface. These creatures—shrimp, flounder, crab, sting rays, and eels—are a little woozy due to the lack of oxygen, so they literally swim up to the shore so you can catch them!

Something we did not know until we probed further was that most jubilees occur during predawn hours. For those of you keeping score at home, that would be anywhere from 2:00 a.m. to 5:00 a.m. I usually reserve this time of night for sleeping rather than observing oceanic marvels. Also, jubilees occur more often in pockets rather than along the whole stretch of the eastern shore, meaning that they are mainly isolated events.

Furthermore, since not many people are walking the shores of the beach at that time of night, the only way one can hear about a jubilee is to get on "the list." The list is an unsophisticated phone tree that is haphazard at best about passing the word that a jubilee is occurring. Given the conditions surrounding the event, you can see how actually being a part of a jubilee is hit or miss!

Imagine my jubilation (pardon the pun) when I got the call one sultry summer night at around ten thirty in the evening. I couldn't believe my luck. A jubilee before the predawn hours! I flew from the back of the house to gather my wife and kids and head down to the bay. "There's a jubilee!" I yelled.

"Shhh!" my wife scolded. "It's a school night. The kids are already asleep."

"But it's a jubilee," I said, as if she didn't hear me the first time. She just looked at me. She had her Mickey Mouse pajama bottoms on and a Seaside T-shirt. "Nobody's going, are they?"

She shook her head. "Have fun. Go."

My first jubilee was just as I had pictured. I had heard from the old timers that the fish were groggy, almost in a trance. Sure enough, flounder by the dozens were slowly making their way to the shore, swimming over a host of crab crawling in the shallow water. A few eels slithered underneath the pier where I stood. I laughed out loud. Christy would not have liked that at all. For a good twenty minutes, I watched this unnatural spectacle in amazement.

As I walked back to my car, a bittersweet feeling overwhelmed me. I was glad that I got to experience the jubilee, but I was profoundly sad that I wasn't able to share a memory with my family. Looking back, I should have roused the boys and faced Christy's scorn. It would have been worth it.

It made me stop and think ... How many people will miss out on the jubilee of heaven just because I didn't make an effort to ask them to come along with me?

Week 6:	Praise!
Reflection:	We have life abundant. We should be spreading it.
Scripture:	2 Timothy 4:17–18

But the Lord stood at my side and gave me strength, so that through me the message might be fully proclaimed and all the Gentiles might hear it. And I was delivered from the lion's mouth. The Lord will rescue me from every evil attack and will bring me safely to his heavenly kingdom. To him be glory for ever and ever. Amen.

Pray/Meditate:

1. The people in our world are much like the fish in a jubilee—slowly swimming to their deaths. Does that bother us? Does it stir our compassion? Pray that it will.

2. Timothy was probably one of the last books the apostle Paul wrote. The end of his ministry and his life was near, yet he approached it confidently, knowing that he "fought the good fight." Pray that God will lead you into the fight so that one day you can say, as Paul did, "Now there is in store for me a crown of righteousness, which the Lord, the righteous judge, will award to me on that day."

3. Pray that the final days of the Go Fish Project will provide further opportunity us to draw others to the jubilee!

5:10 Task: E-mail info@gofishproject.com with suggestions, ideas, and helpful hints that could make this experience even better!

Holy Compassion, Batman!

In case you aren't aware of this, all boys go through a superhero phase. Birthday parties, Halloween costumes, and pajamas all present little boys with a chance to enter their alter egos of Superman, Batman, or Spider-Man. Word to the wise, though … keep an eye on the Darth Vader kids.

My mother has a picture of her five "superhero" grandsons when they were two, three, four, five, and six sitting in a row on her fireplace. They all are wearing homemade purple capes because my mother wanted them to feel "authentic" as they patrolled her house for the bad guys. Don't you love grandmothers? Unbelievable!

Speaking of unbelievable, the city of San Francisco recently came together for a little boy named Miles Scott who wanted to be a superhero. Miles—a leukemia patient—approached the Make-a-Wish Foundation with his desire to be Batkid for a day, and boy, did they deliver!

Make-a-Wish went public with Miles's story, and it caught fire on social media. Hundreds, if not thousands, of people got in on the wish. The day began with the *San Francisco Chronicle* newspaper dedicating the entire front page to Batkid with stories written by … you guessed it, Clark Kent, Lois Lane, and Perry White. At 9:30 a.m., the San Francisco police chief interrupted regular TV programming asking the city to help find Batkid and bring the bad guys to justice.

Upon hearing the plea from the chief, Miles—uh, I mean Batkid—went into action. He thwarted a bank robbery by the Riddler, rescued a damsel in distress from a cable car in Hyde Park, and then took a break for lunch. While enjoying his burger, Batkid glanced over to see hundreds of people jumping up and down, trying to get his attention. Apparently the villainous Penguin was attempting to kidnap the San Francisco Giant's mascot—Lou Seal—and take him from the city. Luckily, Batkid foiled the plot and ended his day on the steps of city hall, where the police chief thanked him and San Francisco's mayor gave him a key to the city while thousands gathered around him to cheer.

Batkid's exploits did not escape the US attorney's office, who issued a news release announcing the arrest of the Riddler and Penguin. Even President Obama got in on the action, congratulating Miles for a job well done.

"This is one that we thought of as a great opportunity for people to share in the power of a wish so they can see how it affects not only the children and their families, but also the other people involved," Jen Wilson, marketing and promotions manager for Make-a-Wish in San Francisco, told ABCNews.com. "It has a big impact on many people."[36]

So if you are wondering what Go Fish Project might look like, there you have it—in San Francisco, California. In its purest form, Go Fish is just about people gathering together to address a need. Jesus himself said in Matthew 9:12, "Go and learn what this means: I desire mercy and not sacrifice." Go Fish Project goes one step further. It addresses a need with the only true permanent solution—the love of Jesus Christ. Only in him can we find the truth, love, hope, and purpose to fill the void in our souls.

When Christians go in love, we resemble our namesake.

Go ... in love.

Go Fish.

---

36 Batkid's Make-a-Wish transforms San Francisco into Gotham; accessed at http://abcnews.go.com/US/batkids-make-transformed-san-francisco-gotham/story?id=20899254. November 2013. Accessed August 28, 2014.

Week 6:	Praise!
Reflection:	Compassion conquers complacency.
Scripture:	Matthew 25:31–36

"When the Son of Man comes in his glory, and all the angels with him, he will sit on his glorious throne. All the nations will be gathered before him, and he will separate the people one from another as a shepherd separates the sheep from the goats. He will put the sheep on his right and the goats on his left. Then the King will say to those on his right, 'Come, you who are blessed by my Father; take your inheritance, the kingdom prepared for you since the creation of the world. For I was hungry and you gave me something to eat, I was thirsty and you gave me something to drink, I was a stranger and you invited me in, I needed clothes and you clothed me, I was sick and you looked after me, I was in prison and you came to visit me.'"

Pray/Meditate:

1. Are we looking for the Miles Scotts around us? Who is in need of love? Pray for opportunities to address the needs of the hungry, the thirsty, the stranger, the unclothed, and the sick.

2. One day Miles Scott will outgrow his childhood dreams of Batkid, and he will need a real superhero to save him from the evil in this life. Only Jesus can do that. Pray that our hearts will be as tender for a five-year-old with leukemia as our next-door neighbor or the obnoxious guy who cut us off in traffic yesterday.

3. As you finish your first Go Fish Project, pray specifically for your next opportunity. I promise you, it is out there ... waiting for someone to demonstrate the love of Christ.

5:10 Task:	Go to YouTube and type in "Official Batkid Video Make-a-Wish." Imagine if Christians rallied together to demonstrate the love of Christ like this to a sick and needy world ...

Appendix

Team Inventory Work Sheet

Name	Personal/Professional Experience	How to use during GFP
John Doe (example)	- accountant, proficient Excel, Word - previous mission project work - friend of two couples in target area - can paint, minor carpentry	Organize team, draft a plan Direct resources to project May use network to help GFP Home repair and renovation
Go Fish Project Partner:		

Appendix

Team Meeting 3

Go Fish Project Organizational Worksheet

The primary need our project will address: _____

Start date of project: _____

End date of project: _____

Work dates to complete project: _____

List of resources needed and team member resonsible for:

Resources/Items for Project	Team Member Responsible

Resources/Items for Project	Team Member Responsible

Appendix

Team Meeting 3
Go Fish Project Organizational Worksheet

Specific Tasks for Go Fish Project	Team Member Responsible

Appendix

Team Meeting 4
Preparation for the Lord's Supper

The Lord's Supper is designed to be a simple yet reverent event in the lives of Christians. Early Christians met in homes and experienced the event as part of fellowship and reflection. That being said, over the years, different denominations have established different ways to celebrate communion. Today, choose the way your group is comfortable to remember Christ's sacrifice. Feel free to use your creativity to make this a meaningful event for the participants.

Preparation

Materials Needed: grape juice, cups, pitcher, bread, napkins, chairs, table, a Bible to read Scripture

Optional: serving trays, candles, music

Setting: While we want the observation of the Lord's Supper to be reverent, we also want it to be relaxed and informal. Remember, you will have your partner(s) from the community with you, so we want this to be a warm and encouraging spiritual event for them.

Set the chairs up in a circle to encourage a more relaxed, intimate feel.

Designate someone to lead the group during the celebration of the Lord's Supper.

Once your group is ready to move to this portion of your team meeting, have the leader designated to administer the Lord's Supper transition into a time of reflection and thankfulness with a prayer.

Appendix

Team Meeting 4

Administration of the Lord's Supper, Leader's Script

We are celebrating the Lord's Supper for two reasons. First, it's because Jesus commanded us to do this in remembrance of him as often as we gather. Second, nothing better demonstrates his love for us more than observing the Lord's Supper. It reminds us of the sacrifice of his body and blood for the atonement of our sins. As we reflect upon his suffering tonight, let us remember to demonstrate the love of Christ to others as we go out into the community.

Luke 22:15 tells us that Jesus said on the night of the first Lord's Supper, "I have eagerly desired to eat this Passover with you before I suffer."

Given the circumstances, what do you think was going through Jesus' mind that night as he was gathered together with his friends? (Give time for group to reflect and answer.)

We don't know all that Jesus said in the upper room, but much of it is recorded in the gospels. When it came time to eat the meal, Jesus used the opportunity to symbolize the new covenant that was established the following morning on the cross. As we take the elements, let us remember that sacrifice. (Prepare the bread and juice. Pause as you read Luke 22:19–21, allowing for members to take each of the elements.)

After Jesus ate with the disciples, he took a basin of water and towel and washed his disciples' feet. (Read John 13:3–7.) Besides establishing the new covenant that night, what did Jesus want them to remember from these verses? Why was that important to the disciples in the coming days, weeks, and months? Why is it important to our group as we go out into our community?

As the discussion finishes, transition back to step 5 to conclude team meeting 4.